DAVY CROCKETT
Legendary Frontier Hero

His True Life Story
And The Fabulous
Tall Tales Told About Him

by
Walter Blair

Lincoln-Herndon Press Inc.
Springfield, Illinois

CONTENTS

ILLUSTRATIONS

AUTHOR'S
ACKNOWLEDGEMENTS

The following individuals and institutions were most helpful in assembling the photographs and other materials for this book on the life of Davy Crockett:

Natalie Wright, Director of the University of Tennessee Press, Knoxville, Tennessee.

The Reference Staff of the New York Public Library, New York City, New York.

William H. Richter, Assistant Archivist, Public Service, The General Libraries, University of Texas at Austin, Texas.

Kathleen Gee, Curator of the Harry Ransom Humanities Research Center, The University of Texas at Austin, Texas.

Janine Hall, Secretary, together with Fran Schell, Chief Reference Librarian Tennessee State Library and Archives, Knoxville, Tennessee.

The Lincoln Library of Springfield, Illinois, particularly the staff of the Interlibrary Loan Department and the Reference Department.

i

Davy Crockett, Statesman
Watercolor portrait by Anthony Lewis De Rose.
Courtesy of the New York Historical Society,
New York City

PREFACE

Walter Blair is a man of many parts. A long-time English professor at the University of Chicago, he has spent a goodly portion of his life immersed in the study of America's folkways, its language, its stories, and most of all its humor. A shelf-full of Blair books warrants the claim that he helped "discover" indigenous American humor, at least in the sense of opening it up for close examination and preservation. He has looked in every nook and cranny of our past for new stories and tales, and these yield unexpected insight in Blair's retelling.

Davy Crockett first attracted Blair's attention in the 1930's. Since then, he has written much about Crockett. He has argued that the real Davy Crockett comes to us bedecked in legends, and that there are at least six Crocketts we have to sort through to understand the real one and to appreciate the lore about him. Blair has also argued that there is a large degree of similarity between the humor of and about Crockett and that of Abraham Lincoln, which is certainly true. Lincoln had to know about Davy Crockett and his richly embellished story. Both shared a backwoods idiom and delighted in wacky stories. Finally, no one more than Walter Blair has

iii

helped other scholars understand the nuances of the Crockett legend and its history from even before Crockett himself died to Walt Disney's evocative recreation of the story.

Behind the legend stands an immensely complicated man. Born and raised on the frontier, Crockett spent most of his life hunting game and restlessly searching out new opportunities. As a youth he ran away from home. Later, he courted and married, raising a family for which he adequately provided. He fought Indians in frontier battles and killed more game, especially bears, than one can easily comprehend in the 20th century.

Davy Crockett, however, was no simple backwoodsman. He seemed to be a born leader; certainly he was respected by his peers for his courage, directness, and honesty. He became involved first in local Tennessee politics in the mid-1820's and soon found himself a United States Congressman. He was to clash with President Andrew Jackson over Indian policy—Crocket objected to Indian removal in 1830—and this caused a severe setback in his political career. In fact, Crockett's own autobiography, *Narrative of the Life of David Crockett of the State of Tennessee*, was an attempt to regain political stature. In it Crockett refers several times to "President Crockett." Charles and Mary Beard argued many years ago that: "The politics of the frontier was the politics of the backwoodsmen; and if a type of the age is needed . . . it may well be David Crockett, whose autobiography is one of the prime human documents for the American epic yet to be written." Davy Crockett, one might say, is the heir to Benjamin Franklin and the ancestor of Henry Adams. He stands at a critical juncture in the emergence of the American character.

Crockett's story has in turn reverberated with that of American culture in strange ways. For the two decades after his death in 1836 Davy Crockett was an enormously popular folk hero as an Alamo martyr. For years his ghost inspired the Crockett *Almanacs*. After that he slowly slipped into obscurity. For a brief period in the latter decades of the 19th century Crockett recovered some of his popularity, but by the centennial of his death only Walter Blair and a few crusty scholars knew or cared much about this seminal figure in our past. One can argue, however, that certain images in consciousness never die; they come too early ever to be eradicated. Surely Davy Crockett, real and imagined, in this sense awaited discovery. Thus the Crockett whom Walt Disney (re-) created in the 1950's brought alive a distantly familiar hero. Now it seems Crockett slumbers again in our minds. Perhaps this book will change that.

Walter Blair's fine work in this timeless biography of Davy Crockett is to make both the historical figure and the tall tale frontiersman accessible to ordinary readers. The learning behind the seemingly effortless prose in this book is vast and deep. The historical biography is carefully based on what can be actually verified about Davy Crockett, but he also retells the imaginative popular fiction about him. The heresay he includes is clearly identified. Blair's telling of the Crockett story is lively, enormously readable, and fun. We are indebted to him for keeping alive this piece of our past. This book, now again in print and paperback, brings both the true and the legendary Davy Crockett back where they belong: in focus and on the minds of Americans everywhere.

Charles B. Strozier
Professor of History
Sangamon State University
Springfield, Illinois

THE HISTORICAL RECORD

1786—August 17, David Crockett, who would become famous as "Davy Crockett," was born in a log cabin at the juncture of the Limestone and Nolachucky Rivers, near present-day Rogersville, Tennessee, to Mr. and Mrs. John Crockett. Ancestors on his father's side of the family were French and Irish, on his mother's (Hawkins') side, English. David had two sisters, and was the fifth of six brothers.

1794—The family moved to the mouth of Cove Creek in Greene County. John Crockett and a partner built a mill on Cove Creek. A spring freshet swept the mill away, and the family moved to Jefferson County.

1796—John opened a tavern on the Knoxville to Washington road.

1798—Hard pressed financially, John hired out Davy, aged twelve, to Jacob Siler. Siler, driving a herd of cattle, had stopped at the tavern on his way to Virginia. The boy worked for him in Virginia, three miles from Natural Bridge.

1798 or early 1799—Badly treated by Siler, Davy ran away from him and returned home.

1799–1802—Punished for playing hookey from school, Davy ran away. After three years of wandering, he again returned home.

1803–1804—Davy went to school part time for about six months, a total of 100 days or so in all. He also helped as a farmhand.

1805—In October, Davy was jilted by Margaret Elder.

1806—Davy married Polly Finley in Jefferson County, Tennessee, in August, and worked on a small rented farm.

1811—Davy and his family, now including two sons, moved to Lincoln County, near the Alabama border, at the head of Mulberry Fork of the Elk River. There, Davy became famous as a great hunter.

1813–1815—Davy and his family lived on a homestead ten miles below Winchester. After September, 1813, and during 1814 and part of 1815, Davy was away from home serving two enlistment periods. When he was mustered out in March, 1815, he was a sergeant.

1815—Polly Crockett died in the summer.

1816—Davy married Elizabeth Patton, a young widow with two children. While exploring a newly opening frontier area, Davy suffered a bad attack of malaria. Elizabeth got news that he had died, so was astonished when he returned home.

1817—The family moved to the head of Shoal Creek in Lawrence County. Davy's neighbors informally chose him to be a magistrate, and in November, by official state action, he was made a justice of peace, to serve until the end of 1819.

1818—Davy was elected lieutenant colonel-commandant of

the 57th Militia Regiment in Lawrence County, and town commissioner for Lawrenceburg.

1821–1822—Having been elected in 1820 to the Tennessee State Legislature, Davy served until the winter of 1822. During the winter, 1821-1822, he explored the Obion River country. After a spring flood wrecked the Crockett mills and distillery on Shoal Creek, the family moved to a homestead on the Obion River.

1823—Crockett was elected to the Tennessee State Legislature by his new constituency.

1826—During the spring, Davy started to run two boats with cargoes of staves to New Orleans. The boats were wrecked, and he narrowly escaped drowning. In Memphis, he met Major J. B. Winchester, who urged him to enter national politics, and loaned him money to campaign. Davy helped oversee the building of several local roads.

1827–1831—Davy was elected to serve in the twentieth and twenty-first Congress. Although originally he was a strong supporter of Andrew Jackson, beginning in 1828, he was increasingly in opposition to him. In 1830, he spoke eloquently against the Indian removal bill. Thanks largely to Washington gossip and newspaper items about him, Davy became a national celebrity. In 1831, a popular play by James Kirk Paulding, revised by W. B. Bernard, was produced. It featured Nimrod Wildfire, widely recognized as a comic caricature of Crockett. With James K. Hackett, a leading comedian, as Wildfire, it would be produced frequently not only in America but also in England during more than two decades. Running for his term in Congress in 1831, Davy was defeated.

1833—A book, *Life and Adventures of Colonel David Cro-*

ckett of West Tennessee, also published as *Sketches and Eccentricities of Colonel David Crockett of West Tennessee*, was published and sold widely. Pretty surely, the author was not Davy but Mathew St. Clair Clarke, clerk of the House of Representatives.

1833–1835—When Davy again ran for Congress, he was elected. He served in the twenty-third session. In 1834, aided by Kentucky Congressman Thomas Chilton, Davy wrote and published *A Narrative of the Life of David Crockett of Tennessee*, recognized as his autobiography.

In 1834, Crockett made a speaking tour through New England and the East.

1834–1855—First in Nashville, Tennessee, later in a number of widely scattered cities, forty-five annual *Crockett Almanacks* were widely distributed. In addition to calendars and forecasts, these contained autobiographical passages, frontier tall tales, and reports on Western life that were ascribed to Crockett, although he had nothing to do with the publications. These built the legendry about him.

1835—Crockett was defeated when he again ran for Congress. *An Account of Colonel Crockett's Tour of the North and Down East*, probably written by William Clark, and a satirical *Life of Martin Van Buren*, probably by A. S. Clayton, were published under Crockett's name. When Halley's comet appeared, a number of newspapers printed stories claiming that President Jackson had asked Davy to wring off its tail. On November 1, Crockett and some friends left for Texas. During the winter, he explored the Red River Valley.

1836—Early in January, Crockett took a Red River steamer to Natchitoches, Louisiana. By January 5, he was in nearby

Nacogdoches, Texas, where he made a speech containing his account of his last campaign: "I told the people of my District that, if they saw fit to reelect me, I would serve them as faithfully as I had done; but if not, they might go to hell, and I would go to Texas . . . . and here I am." In February, Davy went to San Antonio de Bexar, Texas, where he joined the forces in the fortress called the Alamo. On February 23, Mexican forces under the command of General Antonio Lopez Santa Anna launched a siege against the fortress. The Alamo fell on March 6, and Davy Crockett lost his life.

THE AUTHENTIC DAVY CROCKETT
Oil painting by John Gadsby Chapman.
Courtesy of the Harry Ransom Humanities Center
Art Collection, The University of Texas at Austin.

THE TRUTH AND THE LEGEND

READERS will soon see, I believe, that in this book I've done my best to tell the gospel truth about Davy Crockett. I've taken some of the facts from the best histories or biographies or documents. I've taken some from letters Davy wrote and from books he had a hand in writing. Often, I've told about things that took place pretty much in the words Davy himself used.

There's another Davy Crockett in this book, too, also a very interesting and likable fellow. This is the frontier hero or the amusing character who was a legend, as they call it, in Davy's own day and who still is a legend in ours. This Davy Crockett sprang up because Davy was the sort of man people, including Davy, naturally tell stories about, and because some folks in his day and ours have tended to stretch things or even invent them when they talked or wrote about him. These people weren't solemn historians the way I am, and you never can be sure how much of a try they made at getting things straight.

Well, to help readers winnow out the sober truth, the biography, and the history from the legends, if they want to, I've taken pains to say so plainly whenever I've picked up things from people who tended to talk tall. I've put the responsibility on these people (the way historians have a way of doing). In cases like that I tell you "the neighbors say," "it's said," "the story goes," "a fellow tells us" and the like.

What I claim is that both truth and legend belong in a proper book about this famous American. For both help show what the man was like and what his heroic and human story has meant to his countrymen.

W.B.

Truth and Legend—1837 Almanack

DAVY CROCKETT, FRONTIER HERO
Woodcut from DAVY CROCKETT'S ALMANACK:
1838

PILLOWED ON A WILDCAT SKIN

ANYONE WHO WANTS a brief statement, making clear who Davy Crockett was, at the start, will find Davy once put the whole thing in a nutshell. This, so the story goes, was in a modest little speech he made in Congress, after he'd been elected by his district in Tennessee.

"Mr. Speaker: The gentleman from Massachusetts talks about summing up the merits of the question, but I'll sum up my own.

"In one word, I'm a screamer. I've got the roughest racking horse, the prettiest sister, the surest rifle and the ugliest dog in the district. My father can whip any man in Tennessee, and I can lick my father. I can give any man on this floor two hours start, and outspeak him.

"I can run faster, dive deeper, stay under longer, and come up drier than any man this side of the Big

5

Swamp. I can outgrin a panther and outstare a flash of lightning, tote a steamboat on my back and play at rough and tumble with a lion, with a kick now and then from a zebra."

Now you take a genius, or an amusing man, or a hero. It's pretty hard to explain him. And when one man is all three of these tucked into one skin, it's more or less impossible. Nobody who knows much about Davy, or who has read this speech, can argue that he wasn't all three. Well, how did he get that way?

My best guess is that he got a good start and, after that, his character and talents and training and adventures took over and made him great.

The start came when Davy and Tennessee got together. Davy was born in Tennessee and he grew up there, too.

You talk to anyone born in Tennessee, and he'll be the first to admit that being born in Tennessee is the best beginning anyone can have. If he grew up there, he may also admit that growing up in Tennessee is sure to finish the job.

The way nations and states fought for the right to own Tennessee from the time someone first noticed the place, you might think they had a hunch that Davy Crockett was going to be born there and they all wanted him for a citizen. The Spaniards wanted

Tennessee. The French wanted her. The English wanted her. It was only after a long and hard tussle that the English latched onto her—signed, sealed and delivered in a treaty in 1763. Then the Americans up and started a Revolution and snatched her from the English.

When the Revolution had ended and the redcoats had sailed back to England, there was North Carolina clutching Tennessee in a firm grip and saying she was simply a bundle of North Carolina counties.

Not much later, on August 17, 1786, Davy Crockett was born in this wild, disputed frontier territory. Four years, nine months and nine days later, Davy's fellow citizens made North Carolina turn Tennessee loose. And six years and six days later, Tennessee became a full-fledged state, and the United States was able to put a sixteenth star on the flag.

It might seem to most of us that Davy was too young to have anything to do with such goings on. That's as may be. Some who knew Davy in those days, though, wouldn't agree to this in a hurry. Because according to them, he began to be outstanding mighty early.

From the way Davy's mother and father lived, you might guess they were just ordinary people. They'd come west from Maryland or Virginia or

North Carolina or some such place, as likely as not, but that was nothing. In those days, everybody out West had come there from one place or another.

Davy's mother and father had a log cabin like any other log cabin. The roof was oak staves held in place by slabs that were laid across them at right angles. The windows, of course, were made out of oiled paper. In the fall, Maw and Paw Crockett would put chinks between the logs, to help keep the cabin warm. In the spring, when the redbud and the dogwood came out, they'd knock away the chinks so that light and air could come into the cabin during the hot season.

Inside, the cabin looked like any other. The floor was made of wide planks, held in place on the puncheons with wooden pegs. The table top was a split slab, and the round legs were set in auger holes in the floor. For chairs, they used blocks or three-legged stools. Beds were made with poles interlaced with strips of bark.

Hanging on the wall were gourds of all shapes and sizes for keeping salt, soap, lard and such stuff. Then there were meat and vegetables drying up there in the rafters.

All this, you might say, was as common as an old shoe. Well, it was.

But the Crocketts weren't ordinary people—far

8

from it. They had great talents, and they lived in a great place.

A good many years later, when Davy was older and his parents, it happened, were also, Davy, if you can believe claims that were made told about them in these words:

"My daddy is a true sample of white oak. His bark's a little wrinkled, but his trunk is so all flinty hard that you can strike fire from it with a sledge hammer. He can still look the sun in the face without sneezing. He can still grin a hailstorm into sunshine.

"My maw, she's a glorious girl for her age. She can still jump a seven-rail fence backwards, dance a hole through a double oak floor, spin more wool than one of your steam mills, and smoke a bale of Kentucky tobacco in her corncob pipe in a week. She can crack walnuts for her great-grandchildren with her front teeth, and laugh a horse blind. She can cut down a gum tree ten feet around, and steer it across Salt River with her apron for a sail and her left leg for a rudder."

If he really said this, Davy may have stretched the facts here, as at times he did. Regardless, this suggests his family was unusual.

At the time Davy was born, his father and mother lived in the Nolachucky River Valley, in Tennessee.

9

It was a rather dangerous place, since Indians were on all sides. The Cherokees were on the east along the borders of Virginia and North Carolina. The Creeks were to the south. The Chickasaws were to the west. This left the North, where Kentucky was, but that wasn't very safe. No Indians *lived* there, to be sure, but many fierce animals and Kentuckians did, and Indians from any neighboring tribe were likely to go there to hunt.

But Tennessee was luckily a very healthy place, and anyone living there got built up, it was claimed, so he or she could cope with almost anything.

Tennessee was a place where the soil went down to the center of the earth, and Government gave you title to every inch of it. You could tell the soil was rich because if you went and dug a good-sized hole, and then threw the dirt back into it, you couldn't get all the dirt back into the hole.

The soil was so rich that you had only to kick a dent in the ground with your heel, drop a kernel of corn into the dent, and the corn would grow without your doing a lick of work. Some places, the ground was so covered with wild strawberries that when a boy walked through them, the squished juice would redden his legs to the knees. Other places, the wild pea vines were matted so thick that a horse couldn't make his way through them very handily. If he took a running jump and tried, he was likely to end up with his legs, his neck, his tail and his ears sprawled around every which way, sort of like an octopus.

"If I just sniff the air of the Nolachucky Valley," Davy's father said, "it makes me snort like a horse. Why, when I go to church, I've got to take care to breathe light, else I'll interrupt the sermon with snorts."

The story was that, born to such a family in such a place, Davy Crockett was about the biggest baby that ever was and the smartest that ever will be. His Uncle Roarious said right away that he was the yallerest blossom in the family. He looked so fat and healthy that his Aunt Ketinah said it was as much fun just to look at him as it was to eat a meal with all the trimmings.

"Because of his size," a solemn (though at times a bit playful) writer tells us, "Davy was given an oversize cradle made from the shell of an oversize snapping turtle. His pillow was a wildcat skin filled with the down from thirty-three geese and eleven ganders, as near as I can figure it out.

"Sometimes the cradle was rocked by water power from the Nolachucky River. Other times, Uncle Roarious tied the cradle up near the top of a tree, so the wind would swing it about, and Davy could enjoy himself. An alligator skin that the boy's

11

uncle had spread over elk horns on top of the cradle kept the baby safe from rain, hail or snow."

The family, we are told, used to say that they couldn't let Davy stay in the cabin very much, because if he laughed or cried, he did it so loud that it used to set the cider barrels rolling around the cellar.

"The first thing I can remember is a bear's snout," someone claims Davy told him. "It was a great while ago, but I remember how his great long nose looked, just as plain. I was in my cradle, out in the clearing. He poked his snout in under the elkskin and snuffled, the way bears do. He was just going to take a nip out of me, which would have been most uncomfortable. By good luck, my maw saw him. She ran from the cabin and flung a whole bowl of rattlesnake soup on his hinder end.

"At the same minute, I happened to thrash around and hit the bear's snout with my small fist, driving it back about two inches into his head. The bear got very much hence at once, or slightly sooner, and my beauty, if you want to call it that, was unspoiled."

Some say that for a few months Davy drank buffalo milk instead of regular milk, and this made him grow so that soon he was able to eat meat. At mealtime, to get off to a start, he'd eat a whole duck. Then he'd take a big helping of bear's meat and make it fly. For a snack between meals, he had a

Baby Davy—1848 Almanack

habit of taking a sandwich made of half a bear's hind leg and two spareribs in a loaf of bread.

"Of course," they say, "Davy liked bear's meat most when it was fixed just right—salted in a hailstorm, peppered with buckshot, and broiled on a flash of forked lightning."

All this food made him grow.

As time passed, he got older, too.

It was along in here that something happened which he himself was to remember and write down long after:

"My four older brothers, along with a well-grown boy about fifteen years old, named Campbell, and myself were all playing by the river. Next thing I knew, they'd all piled into my father's canoe and put out on the water. I was left on shore alone.

"A little below, there was a fall in the river that went slap right straight down. From where I was I could hear it roar.

"Now my brothers had paddled a canoe many times, and could have got it to go wherever they wanted. But Campbell wouldn't let them have the paddle. Like a fool, he wanted to manage it himself. The way he paddled, with everything going wrong every time he splashed oar into water, I reckon he'd never seen a canoe before. Well, in no time the boat was headed right plump for the falls, stern foremost.

"I started to howl. This wasn't because I was scared; it was because I was so infernal mad that they'd left me on shore. My howl made a fellow that was named Kendall , in a field close by, look up. He saw the danger, and was more worried about it than I was—possibly because he had more sense.

"He started full tilt, and here he came like a canebrake fire. As he ran, he threw off his coat, then his jacket, and then his shirt. He was running so hard, and undressing in such an unusual way, this threw an awful scare into me, so I screamed like a young panther.

"Kendall went ahead with all his might. He plunged in. When it was too deep to wade, he'd swim, and where it was shallow, he went bolting on. And by such work as I never saw another time in my life, he got to the canoe when it was within twenty feet of the falls. The suck was so great there, and the current was so fast, that poor Kendall had a hard time to stop the canoe. But he hung on till he got it stopped, and then lugged it out of danger.

"When they got out, I saw the boys were more scared than I had been. I remember that I took comfort from the thought that they'd been punished for leaving me ashore."

That's Davy's story. Others said they took no stock in it.

15

"Why," they said, "by that time Davy could float down the Nolachucky River or any other river in Tennessee (including the Sequatchie, the Duck, the Cumberland and the Tennessee River), paddling with nothing but an old horn spoon, while all the neighbors cheered. Kendall didn't need to save those young 'uns; Davy could have."

Be that as it may, and in spite of some scares like this young Davy had, Tennessee—as has been hinted—was a fine place for the boy to grow up in. For one thing, there was plenty of room, even for Davy. For another, it wasn't a noisy place: there was peace and quiet a-plenty. There wasn't any sound to speak of at night—just the howls of some wolves now and then, or an old owl moaning, or a few panthers screaming. In the daytime, it was just about as quiet—with a few hundred ravens croaking, maybe, or a woodpecker or two hammering a hollow beech tree, or the whir of a flight of geese, or some settlers shooting a few Indians or varmints, as the case might be.

Finally, it was a good place to grow because Davy's father and mother, not having any help, were busy all the time, and they had to leave this growing business pretty much up to Davy. They couldn't help him, because they had to milk cows, cook the mess, spin the flax, plow the field, plant the crops, pick the corn, dig the potatoes, shoot the bears, and chase the Indians away.

Davy put his mind to growing, and the way he got along was astonishing.

The story goes that when Davy was six years old, he had a dog named Butcher who was as woolly as a sheep and as old and hard as a rock. Davy would climb on Butcher's back, and they'd slash through the canebrake faster than lightning splitting a post.

Maybe it would be spring, and the buttercups and shooting stars would be up, and the bears would be coming out of their winter snoozing places—hollow trees or caves. Coming into the sunshine after all that sleep, they'd have eyes as red as strawberries. They'd be in a bad mood—blinking their eyes and frowning and sort of snarling.

A storyteller tells us: when Butcher smelled out some of these bears, he'd bark and chase them. Davy would screech and the bears, quick as a spark, would nip for a hole in a tree or a cave or any hiding place that was handy. If they didn't make it, it's said, Davy would put a rifle ball between their eyes. (This was when Davy was six, you should notice. The claim that Davy killed a bear when he was only three seems to be one of those wild tales that grow up about great men.)

Having got old enough to chase bears and sometimes to shoot one, Davy had to get educated now like almost any other boy—had to learn all the useful things that would help him get along.

He had to learn to tell when the ice on the rivers would hold him up—whether it meant anything serious or not when it started to make cracking noises. He had to learn to tell directions by looking at the moss on the trees, in case he got misplaced in the forest some time.

He had to learn the signs which foretell the weather—for example:

If the wind doesn't blow on New Year's Day, there'll be a long dry spell come summer. If there's a breeze, there'll be enough rain to make a crop. If there's a regular ripper of a wind, look out for floods next fall.

If the first twelve days of January have pretty weather, the whole year will be mild.

If fawns lose their spots along about mid-July, the fall will be early.

Onion skin . . . mighty thin . . . easy winter . . . comin' in.

Signs of a bad winter are these: a thick breastbone on a wild goose, so when you hold the peeled bone up to the light, the light doesn't shine through; hornets building their nests low on the trees; thick shucks on the corn; a large crop of nuts; crab grass lying flat on the ground.

(You couldn't do much about the weather, of course. But it helped to be forewarned.)

Davy had to learn to make noises like every beast and bird in the woods. It was a handy thing to be able to gobble like a turkey, because that way you could lure a turkey into shooting range. Or if you could bleat like a fawn, maybe a deer would come running to see what the trouble was.

Another thing that made it useful to know how animals or birds sounded was that Indians signaled this way at night under the black trees. They could bark like a wolf, bleat like a deer, gobble like a turkey, hoot like and owl. Usually, by good luck, they weren't perfect. They'd get the tone wrong, or the rhythm of the call and the answer a little off. If they were good, the only thing that worked was being able to notice whether the call came from too low or too high. An owl didn't hoot from the ground as a rule, for instance, and wolves hardly ever sat up in a tree to do their howling.

If a boy in those days got a failing mark in lessons like this, the blamed thing might be made by a tomahawk, which was inconvenient.

Speaking of tomahawks: like all the boys in Tennessee, Davy had to learn how to throw the tomahawk. The chief thing to know was that a tomahawk would make a certain number of turns at a certain distance. If you learned it from the wrong distance, it wouldn't strike with the blade. At five steps, though, it would strike with the blade and the handle would point down, at seven and a half, it would strike with the handle up, and so on. Davy learned to judge distances with his eye, and soon he could walk through the woods and flip the tomahawk anywhere and any way he wanted it to light.

The exercise made Davy grow even bigger.

The story was that if any of the neighbors wanted to sink tree posts into the bed of the Nolachucky River or the brown Mississippi for bridge piers, all they had to do was lower them down into the mud and then ask Davy to jump on them. He'd step from post to post all the way across the river, making even the tallest posts zip down quicker than half a wink. He'd have to swim back, of course, because if he stepped on the posts twice, he sank them clear out of sight and, what's more, got his feet wet. Swimming back was easy enough for Davy, though, because even at this age he was a ripsnorter of a swimmer.

These facts, if you want to believe them such, were told by people back in Davy's day, and some were written down in books with footnotes and indexes and the like. We come now to a few facts we're less sure about.

"Along when he was about eight," it is claimed the family said, "Davy shed his first teeth. These were saved up and used with mortar to make our parlor fireplace."

This may be so, of course. But a few things about the story make me suspect it may be a little inaccurate. For one thing, I don't think that the Crocketts had a parlor fireplace at that time, although they did have one two years later. For another thing, a boy as young as Davy probably wouldn't have teeth quite that big. Finally, so far as is known, no one— up to this day—ever saw that fireplace.

I'm inclined to think that if the family said this, they were joking. They did joke every now and then, you know.

2

THE GREATEST HUNTER
IN TENNESSEE

DURING THE NEXT few years, Davy got his full growth.

To finish up his training, the Crocketts had the best marksmen and hunters in the valley teach the boy all they knew about shooting, which was plenty. Many a good marksman in those days could stand fifty yards from a burning candle on a dark night and "snuff" it; that is, make his bullet touch the flame without putting it out. From the same distance, many could "bark" squirrels—clip the bark from beneath their feet and make them tumble from a branch. Some could hit a small bird on the wing with a rifle shot.

Along with his lessons, Davy figured out some ideas of his own. After he'd worked and worked to learn, he finally made up a rule for the best way to shoot. The rule was:

23

Be sure you're right, and then go ahead and pull the trigger.

When the leaves were yellow and the sunsets were red and the break of day was gray, that was the best time for hunting. The deer shed his summer suit and put on a winter gray and blue one that would match the scenery better. The elk readied up his antlers—dropped that soft velvet covering and made them hard and white. The bear, fattened up with berries, began to get a little sleepy, maybe, but was wakened easily, at top strength and full of fight.

That was when Davy would make his way through the woods, following his pack of hunting dogs. The lead dog knew a bear's ways as well as a horse-jockey knows a horse's. He always barked at the right time, bit at the exact place, and whipped without getting a scratch. The other dogs were almost as smart. It was hard to tell whether they were made to hunt bear or whether bear were made to be hunted by them.

Davy and his dogs and his rifle, along with his rule for shooting, were unbeatable. Most seasons, it wouldn't take him long to shoot a regular mess of bears and take them home to the family.

Word got around among the settlers that Davy could outhunt any man in the district. So after a while a good many other families got so they'd have him do the hunting for them, too. It's said he wouldn't shoot any turkeys for them, because he shot nothing less than forty-pound turkeys (which were rather scarce), and these he saved for his family. But any time a family wanted a cord or two of bears, he'd oblige, and the family would be fixed for the winter.

Before he went after any bear, he could always tell how big it would be by studying the claw marks on trees. It would stand up as tall as it could and make its scratch on the bark—just why, I've no idea. But noticing a little thing like that, Davy could decide beforehand whether or not a bear was worth the time and trouble it would take to kill him.

Just to show you what a good hunt was like, I've dug up a story Davy told about one. It was like the others, except that he said it was the toughest bear hunt he ever had. This is the story, pretty much in his own words:

"When the time came (as it often did) when I couldn't stand it any longer without a bear hunt, I got a friend, a tent, my pack horses and my dogs and set out. We went down toward the Mississippi, to the Shakes country—so called because there'd been some earthquakes there—where bears were plentiful. On a trip like this I like the wilderness best, where I won't be disturbed except by a few wild animals trying to kill a fellow.

"We got there, raised our tent, stored away our provisions, and went ahead. We started off fine, killed plenty of game to suit us in a few days, and fetched it to the tent and salted it away.

"About sunset one evening, after a hard day, we were stumbling into camp with a heavy pack of meat on each of our pack horses. Of a sudden I heard our dogs make a warm start, and saw them follow old Whirlwind, my lead dog, up a hollow. I knew from the way they sang out they'd started a big *he* bear. I leaped off my horse, told my friend to take him and the pack horses to camp, and followed the dogs.

"I went ahead with all my might for a while, and all the time it was getting darker and colder. Every little while I'd get tangled in vines, or stumble over logs, or fall into one of the big cracks made by the earthquake. Of course, I was mortal scared I'd bust old Betsy (which was the name of my gun) to smithereens or something smaller. But I knew I had to keep in hearing of the dogs now or get lost.

"After a time in the dark, I splashed into a wide knee-deep creek. It took the breath right out of me, it was so cold, and I was hot enough to sizzle. I sloshed across, then stood and listened. I figured my dogs had either treed the bear or brought him to a stop, since their barking stayed in one place. I tell you what, I was mighty glad of it, for by now I was dribbling sweat and icy water like a stove barrel.

"I pushed toward the noise. The creek bank was slippery and too steep to climb. So I had to squidge down the creek a ways to a hollow, go up there, and circle back.

"At first it was so dark I couldn't have seen a mountain two inches in front of my nose. After panting a few minutes, though, I could make out a tree against the sky, with the dogs below barking and jumping at its branches. I stepped closer and saw the tree was a big forked poplar, with a lump that was the bear sitting in the fork. The lump was a black spot against a charcoal sky, hardly plain enough to draw a bead on.

"'Well,' says I, 'there's nothing for it but to shoot by guess.'"

"So I aimed the gun, though I was still fluttering from all the running, and fired away. The sound of the bear thumping on the ground made me hope I'd killed him; but the way he and the dogs started scuffling all around me, I soon knew I hadn't. The furred, hard bodies brushed and pushed against me from every side. I staggered around, hard put to it not to get knocked down.

"I dropped Betsy, since I couldn't load her in the

midst of that mixup any more than a man could thread a needle while riding on a three-legged horse. I took the big butcher knife out of my belt, and staggered some more, bound and determined if the bear grabbed me—or if I sighted the bear—I'd make use of it. But in the miserable dark, except for one white dog I could make out now and then, all I could see was a black blob sort of like spilled ink only much more active.

"Then they were gone from around me, and the noise seemed to be coming right out of the ground. The bear had got into an earthquake crack. I could tell nothing about him except where the biting end of him was: this I could tell by the yelps of my dogs.

"I took my gun, loaded her, and pushed the muzzle around in the crack till I thought I had it against the main part of his body. I fired, and soon discovered that if I'd hit the varmint, it hadn't been in the right place. He jumped out of the crack and the dogs after him, and they were soon battling too close to me for comfort. They knocked my gun out of my hands, and then were good enough to plop back into the crack again, for which I was grateful.

"I could tell by the way my dogs sang out, they were mighty tired. Again I found by the yelps the way the bear was laying, and I looked for old Betsy to pepper him again. I couldn't find her; but I did find a stick. Thinking of nothing that was more fun, I started punching him with the stick.

"'Well,' says I, 'he doesn't seem to mind that much. Maybe I can get down in the crack, and annoy him with my knife.'

"This was much sooner said than done. I thought about it a while. It was late at night and very cold. I was thirty miles from any settlement. The only living soul nearby was my friend back at camp, and I didn't know where that was. I knew the bear was in a crack made by the shakes, but how deep it was, and whether I could get out if I got in, I couldn't tell. But the dogs by now sounded so pitiful, I decided to risk it.

"I got up and scrabbled down in the crack behind the bear. Where I landed was about as deep as I am high. I felt mighty ticklish, and wished I was out. I couldn't see a thing in the world, but I had a feeling there were a sight too many critters in that crack. I inched along easily up to him, placed my hand on his rump, then softly felt for his shoulder, just behind which is the best place to stick a bear. He started to turn. I made a quick lunge with my butcher, and thanked my stars that it felt as if it went in right. He threshed around and, not being sure, I couldn't help but feel mighty ticklish. But by the time I scrambled out, everything was getting quiet. Soon my dogs all

29

came out, too, and laid down at my feet, which was the way they always did when a bear was finished.

"Usually when you kill a bear, that's the end. But it wasn't the end that night. It had clouded up now, and was horribly dark. I didn't know the direction of camp. Somehow I didn't take to the idea of messing around with any more vines or creeks, hunting for camp. I made up my mind to stay there until morning.

"I took out my flint and steel and raised a little fire. Soon it was clear, though, that the wood was too cold and wet to burn. Then I noticed that, what with the cold water and my sweat, I was powerful cold. I thought I'd freeze, I was so cold. I was tired, too. But I thought I would do the best I could to save my life, and then, if I died, nobody would be to blame. I jumped up and down with all my might. I threw myself into all sorts of motions. But all this wouldn't do: I felt like an icicle that had fallen into a snow-mound. I had my dogs lie on top of me, but this wouldn't do, either. I got up and groped around in the dark.

"Next thing I knew, I was hugging a tree about two feet through. A notion struck me to climb it. So up I climbed-up thirty feet before I struck a limb. Then I slid down. Time after time I'd climb up to the limbs, and then lock my arms around the trunk and slide down. This would make the insides of my legs and arms feel mighty warm and good. I kept this up till daylight, and how often I climbed that tree and slid down I don't know, but I reckon at least a hundred times. As soon as it was light, I saw before me a tree so slick it looked like every varmit in the woods had been sliding down it for a month of Sundays.

"Getting my bearings, I started out, followed by my dogs, and found the camp. With the bear I'd killed the night before, we had as much meat as we could carry. So we loaded our horses and set out for home."

Davy's story shows how rugged and tough a hunt could be for him. But a story or two yarnspinners told went to show that at times hunting could be very easy for him.

They told of one day when Davy had so many chores to do he hadn't much time for hunting. But the family was low on food. What he decided to do, therefore, was to get as much food as he could as quick as he could. He took along a muzzle loading, double-barreled shotgun, because it scattered more shots.

Down by the Nolachucky River he saw a flock of geese coming along, and he saw a big buck, both at the same time. He waited until the geese had flown to just the right place near the buck, then he raised the gun. But at that very minute he saw a rattlesnake coiled nearby, ready to strike.

Thinking fast, Davy made the shot of his life. He let the buck have one barrel, the flock of geese the other, and he shot the ramrod down the snake's throat.

The geese were in line, of course, so the shot took them one after the other—the whole string of them.

But that wasn't all. The gun kicked so hard that Davy fell into the river, and when he climbed out, every pocket he had was plumb full of fish. These weighed down his coat and pulled so that two buttons popped off.

One hit a bear and the other hit a squirrel—killed them, too.

The result was, because of his quick thinking and great shooting Davy got his hunting over with in a hurry.

Davy, so some writers said, claimed that one easy way he could hunt was by using a grin. They said he could grin any animal—almost—out of countenance. There were two explanations: One was that Davy was mighty ugly when he grinned. (I doubt this, since pictures show that he was a little handsomer, even, than me.) Another explanation was that just as a snake could hypnotize a bird by looking at it, or a grinning possum could scare a raccoon—or a coon, as they call him for short—to death, Davy could grin an animal to death. (This is a better explanation, it seems to me.)

"I discovered long ago," says a story they claim Davy told, "that a coon couldn't stand my grin. I could grin away at one and bring him tumbling from the highest tree. I almost never wasted powder and lead when I wanted one of the critters.

"Well, as I was walking one night a few hundred yards from my cabin, looking around, I saw a coon planted on one of the highest limbs of an old tree. The night was very moony and clear, and my dog Whirlwind was with me; but Whirlwind won't so much as snort at a coon—he's a queer dog that way. So I thought I'd bring the critter down, as usual, with a grin.

"I set myself—and, after grinning at him the usual time, found he didn't come down. I wondered what was the reason—and I took another steady grin at him. He still was there. It made me a little mad; so I felt around and got an old limb about five feet long—and, planting one end on the ground, I placed my chin on the other end and took a rest. I then grinned my best for about five minutes—but the cussed coon hung on.

"So, finding I couldn't bring him down by grinning, I was more set on getting him than ever—because I thought he must be an unusual coon. I went to the cabin, got an ax, came back to the tree, saw the coon still there, and began to chop away. Down came the tree. I ran forward. Well, the coon wasn't to be seen anywhere. Then I found what I'd taken for one was a big bump on the tree with two knotholes in it. I took some pleasure in seeing I'd grinned all the bark off and left the bump as smooth as a mirror, but I still felt tolerable foolish."

People say that after a few years even the animals passed along the word that Davy was the best hunter with his grin or his gun not only in the Nolachucky Valley but also in all of Tennessee and perhaps in Kentucky.

They tell this story to prove it:

Davy was out in the forest one afternoon a little before sunset, and had just come to a place called the Great Gap when he saw a raccoon—a real one this time—sitting all alone in the crotch of a tree. It had the usual look of a coon—gray, ring-tailed, white-eyebrowed, and sort of woebegone, downhearted, dismal, discourged, and sad.

Davy was in a hurry to get home to dinner, and felt he didn't have time to grin and bring the coon down that way. So he put his gun to his shoulder

A Sensible Varmint—1842 Almanack

and was all ready to shoot, when the coon lifted his paw, like a boy at school, and said:

"Is your name by any chance Davy Crockett?"

Says Davy, "You're right for once. That's my name."

"Then," says the animal, "you needn't take any more trouble, because I may as well come down without another word."

And the coon walked down from the tree, as dignified as a gentleman climbing out of a carriage, because he felt he was as good as shot and he said so.

Davy stooped down, patted the little fellow on the head, and said, "I won't hurt a hair on your head, coonie, because you've said as fine a thing about my shooting as ever was said."

"Since you put it like that," says the raccoon, edging off sideways, "I think I'll just walk off right away. It's not that I doubt what you say," the raccoon told Davy, "but you might kind of happen to change your mind."

3

"A POOR
WAYFARING STRANGER"

Y OU SHOULDN'T take it that, while Davy was
growing up and learning to hunt and all, he and his
family stayed long in one place. It seems the Crocketts couldn't get out of the habit of moving.

Moreover, his father, for all his great talents,
couldn't seem to make much of a go of it anywhere.

In spite of the fine soil and the fine climate in the
Nolachucky Valley, the family didn't make out well
there. So they moved over to the mouth of Cove
Creek, where Mr. Crockett went partners with Tom
Galbreath to build a mill. The mill was nearly
finished when, as it happened, the spring freshet
came in extra high and swept the mill away. Then
the family moved over to Jefferson County, where
the old man set up a tavern on the road from
Washington to Knoxville, to take care of the wagoners who traveled that way.

Davy went along with the family, and when he wasn't learning woods lore or hunting, he did what he could to help with the moving and the chores.

About the time he was twelve, though, an old Dutchman named Jacob Siler stopped at the tavern one night. Seems he was driving a herd of cattle to his farm in Virginia, and there were either too many of them or too few of him, so they gave him a lot of trouble. Old man Crockett was pressed for money at the time, so he hired out Davy to go along and help old Siler.

They were hardly out of sight of the clearing when Davy was taken most horribly homesick. He could hardly wait to head back for home, and meant to start back the minute the trip was over. But the Dutchman told him to stay. Well, Davy'd been told to mind his elders, so he stayed. Siler treated him well, but Davy kept getting more and more homesick.

You take a boy of twelve or younger that's never been away from his family overnight, and he can do a better job of being homesick than anybody except a girl that age. Davy appears to have had first-class talents along this line, because he was about twice as unhappy as a kitten in a cold creek. And it didn't help any that he was so far away from home without means to get back.

The result was, when some wagoners he'd known

back in his father's tavern came by the Siler farm, he poured out his troubles in a regular flood.

Now wagoners, take them by and large (and they were mostly large), were about as rough a crowd as you'd find anywhere except on a Mississippi River keelboat. They had to go out and around in all kinds of weather on roads we wouldn't walk a dog on, and stay healthy. It took strong men to ride over roads that were all deep-rutted, muddy, dusty, water-covered, ice-covered or ornery in some other way. With their own two hands, most of them could get a horse back on its feet when the animal had slipped and fallen. For amusement, and to work off cussedness, they'd fight one another or even perfect strangers they met along the way. Usually they'd have an ear or two missing, and their faces had the complexion of country hams and looked as if they'd been used for uncorking bottles, too. In short, they weren't handsome. But in one way, wagoners were like other human beings: some had hearts big as pumpkins, some had hardly any hearts at all, and some were in between. It happened these two fellows were among the best.

"Well," they said, "you aren't bound to stay with Siler forever. We'll be staying the night at a tavern down the road about seven miles. If you can come along by morning, we'll take you home with us."

"I went to bed as usual that night," Davy says, "but sleep seemed to be a stranger to me. I was a wild boy, but I was terrible fond of my folks. I kept remembering the way my father and mother looked, and my sisters and brothers. Then I got to thinking I might be caught if I tried to leave, and that made me even more restless. I felt mighty queer, I can tell you."

Finally, about two o'clock, he slipped out of bed, bundled up his clothes, carefully opened the door and sneaked downstairs, keeping to the part close to the wall so there'd be as few creaks as possible. And every time he made the slightest sound, his heart fluttered up into his mouth.

Outside, he found a storm had thrown about eight inches of snow on the ground. There was no moonlight, of course—just blackness with flurries of snow whirling out of it and pelting him in the face. The big road was half a mile from the house, and mighty hard to find in the dark. Davy made his way to the big road largely by guess, then set out on the seven-mile trip to the wagoners.

"There wasn't," says Davy, "any way to see or feel the road under the deep snow. I never could have followed the thing if I hadn't kept sharp watch on the opening it made in the timber. Whenever I bumped into a tree, I judged I'd got off the road, since there weren't any trees on it that I could remember. After a while the snow was up to my knees, and poison hard to plough through."

He got to the wagoners' camp about an hour before daylight. The wagoners were stirring around, feeding the horses and getting ready to start. By this time the boy was so covered with snow they had to brush him off before they could see who he was.

"It's Davy Crockett," they said then. "Come over by the fire and thaw yourself out, boy. Scald your insides with some of this hot coffee here and we'll be off!"

When Davy was more comfortable, they set out. He enjoyed resting in one of the wagons for a while in spite of the fact that the bumpy roads made the thing jolt as if two or maybe three wheels had lost their rims and were stumbling along on their spokes. Then he got to thinking about being on his way home at last, and soon he was thinking that the wagons were going too slow. They were, too, because it was mighty up-and-down country, and the roads had been fitted to it.

"The thoughts of home began to take over my whole mind," he says. "I almost counted the slow turns of the wheels, and I did keep count of how many more miles we had to go. I kept with the wagoners till we got to the house of John Cole, on the Roanoke River, where we stopped for the night. Then I was so eager I decided to set out on foot and go by myself, as I could travel twice as fast afoot as the wagons were going—or at least I felt I could."

The next day, Davy met a man returning home from market. He had an extra horse, bridled and saddled and ready for a rider. The man asked Davy to climb aboard. This was lucky, because not far ahead was the first crossing of the Roanoke River, where Davy would have had to wade—maybe swim some—through the icy water. Crossing the stream on horseback was much easier and more comfortable.

"About fifteen miles from my father's tavern," says Davy, "we parted, and he took the fork of the road to Kentucky. I trudged on homeward—got there that night. I'm mighty sorry I forgot the name of this gentleman. However, I'll always remember his kindness to a straggling boy who was a complete stranger to him."

Anybody who has ever been homesick, especially around the age of thirteen, can guess how happy Davy was to get home.

He stayed there until the next fall, helping with the chores and the hunting. Then his father made up his mind to send Davy off to school for the first time. The school was a little log cabin, and the master was a pretty stern old codger named Ben Kitchen. Those were days when a teacher couldn't get work unless he could make a hickory stick whir through the air and do a tidy dusting job on a boy's britches, and Ben Kitchen stood high among the teachers. But since Davy preferred his britches dusty, he began to study hard trying to learn his letters and some ciphering.

Then Davy had a falling out with a boy much older and bigger than he was. They couldn't fight right in the schoolhouse, so Davy lay in wait for the other boy after school. When he came along, young Crockett pitched out of the bushes and set on him like a wildcat. Soon the boy yelled "enough," and Davy went on home. He looked a little battered, but no one paid much attention, since it wasn't unusual for him to look battered when he went to school—and even more so when he got home.

"The next morning," says Davy, "I started again for school. But do you think I went? No, indeed. I stayed very clear of it. The trouble was, knowing old Ben Kitchen, I figured he'd probably lick me as bad as I'd licked the boy. Whenever I thought of it, I could almost hear the whish of his rod and feel the whacks of it on my back. I laid out in the woods all day. Then when school let out, I joined my brothers on the way home and persuaded them not to tell on me. I wanted to hide the whole business from my father. I had a notion he might find a rod and do some whishing and whacking himself.

"Things went on this way for several days. But then Kitchen wrote a note to my father, asking where I'd been. This made the old gentleman as savage as a meat ax."

Mr. Crockett called Davy in. "Why haven't you been in school?" he asked him.

"I'm afraid to go," says Davy. "If I'm turned over to old Kitchen, I'll be cooked up to a crackling in little or no time."

"If you don't head for school this minute," says Mr. Crockett, "I'll whop you an eternal sight worse than the master."

"I tried to beg off," says Davy, "but nothing would do but to go to the school. When I dawdled about starting, he pulled up a hickory sapling and broke after me. I streaked away, and soon we were both running at the top of our speed. We had a tolerable tough race for about a mile. But, mind you, it wasn't on the schoolhouse road, because I was trying to get as far t'other way as I could.

"Fortunately for me, about this time I saw a hill just ahead. I made headway over it as fast as a young steamboat going full speed ahead with the current to help. Just over the hilltop, I skinned into some bushes. Here I waited until the old gentleman passed by. He was puffing and blowing as though his steam was high enough to bust his boilers.

"I lay hid till he gave up the hunt and passed me on the way back home. Then I cut out and footed it to the cabin of a fellow I knew a few miles away."

This was Jeff Cheek. Davy'd heard he was about to start off with a drove of cattle he was taking to Virginia. Davy persuaded Jeff to hire him as a helper. They made a powerful hard trip through Chester Gap in the Blue Ridge mountains, but in time ended up in the town of Front Royal. Jeff gave Davy a few dollars, and the boy started home.

He wasn't going to get there, however, as it turned out, for some time. He soon ran out of money and had to work a while for more. Then the same thing would happen all over again. Sometimes he'd be working for wagoners, sometimes for farmers.

One story has it that he worked on a Maryland farm for a while that was about the poorest place that ever was made. When killdeers flew over this place, the tears came to their eyes so they could hardly see. The apples were pitiful little runts of things so sour they made the pigs that ate them howl. The hound dogs were so poor they had to lean against a fence before they could bark. It was hard times working on a farm that fallow, and of course it was always hard times working for wagoners.

But it's not too sure he really wanted to get back home.

"I often thought of home," he says. "I wanted bad enough to be there, in some ways, though not in others. My mind made pictures of the family at table or sitting around a crackling fire in the evening. But then I'd think of old Kitchen, or the race I had with my father, and the hickory sapling he'd carried. And I'd remember how strong the storm of his wrath had been. Then I'd be mortal afraid to go back. I knew my father mighty well, and I knew his anger—once it got to boiling—was likely to hang onto him like a turtle does to a fisherman's toe. Many a time the thought of the promised whipping came right slap down on every thought of home."

Davy went to work as a ploughboy and the next spring, having saved some of his pay—twenty-five cents a day and keep—he decided to go with a wagoner to Baltimore and see what sort of place it was, and what sort of folks lived there. He bought himself some good clothes and gave the wagoner the rest of his savings—about seven dollars—to keep safe for him. They started out with a load of barrels filled with flour.

Near Baltimore, Davy climbed into the wagon to

put on his good clothes, to wear into the city. While he was changing, some road workers came along with their wheelbarrows, laughing and singing. The horses took as much of a scare as if they'd seen two or three ghosts. They reared up and made a sudden wheel around.

The wagon tree broke slap off as short as a pipestem. Snap went both the axletrees all the same time.

"Of all the fiendish flouncing around of flour barrels that ever was seen," says Davy, "I reckon this took the beat. Even a rat would have stood a bad chance in a straight race among them, and not much better in a crooked one. He'd have been ground up as fine as ginger by their rolling over him. But I found if a fellow is born to be hanged, he'll never be drowned, and furthermore, if he's born for a seat in Congress, even flour barrels can't make a mash of him. Because, though I was sure I'd be smashed by those barrels any minute, somehow I came through without a scratch."

When the wagon came to a stop, the wagoner and Davy shifted the flour to another wagon and delivered it. They hauled their broken wagon to a workman's shop in Baltimore to be repaired. They would have to wait two or three days until the job was finished.

One day Davy wandered down to the wharf.

There, for the first time in his life, he saw some great ocean-going ships, far away and beyond the size of flatboats and keelboats he'd seen on the western rivers. They seemed to bristle with masts, and their white sails were flying in the breeze against the blue sky. Strange smells came from them, a mixture of spice and tar and hemp such as Davy had never met up with. Sailors bustled around the decks, talking sailing lingo he'd never heard in all his born life.

After a time, he saw a gang plank leading aboard a fine big ship. He couldn't fight off the temptation to board her. He scuttled aboard and began to snoop around, looking over the rigging and peering into some of the hatches. Before long, he met up with the captain.

"Well, boy," the captain said, "I need a lad like you—been looking for him. How would you like to sign for a voyage to London and back?"

Davy didn't think twice, though he knew no more about sailing than a wild turkey knows about the first seven books of the Bible.

"I'd like it," says he. "I can go and get my clothes and sail at once."

"Step lively then," says the captain. "We cast off tonight."

Young Crockett went back to the wagoner and

told him he wanted his money and his clothes, because he meant to sail to London.

"I'll give you neither," the wagoner answered him back. "What would your folks say if they found I'd let you go to sea? Moreover, I need your help when we leave tomorrow. I'm not giving you your money until I have you back safe in Tennessee."

Davy thought this was very mean, as it was. He tried to get away, but the wagoner kept a close watch over him until they'd left Baltimore and traveled several days on the road.

For some reason (maybe because he felt guilty about the money), the fellow had turned mean. Give him the least chance, and he'd threaten to use his wagon whip to tan the boy's hide.

"Finally," says Davy, "I decided I must leave him. So before daylight one morning, while the fellow was snoring loud as a buzz saw, I got my clothes out of the wagon and cut out. I didn't have a penny, of course, and I had to go on foot."

Things looked pretty dismal until a few miles along the road Davy came up with another wagoner. When he told the man how badly he'd been used, the wagoner was mighty wrathy.

"That fellow's a rat, sure enough!" says the wagoner. "I'll see he gives you back every cent. We'll go back and meet him."

49

"Oh," says Davy, "I'm afraid to go back. He's said again and again he'll use his whip on me."

"Pah!" the wagoner said. "I can handle him. You'll get your money, or I'll whip *him*!" He was a huge, stout fellow and appeared to be as strong as a panther, so he looked as if he could do it.

Well, they turned back and met up with the other fellow about two miles down the road. Davy's new friend leaped down and went over to him.

"You're a rascal," he yelled. "You've treated this boy bad."

"No. It was his fault."

"Didn't he give you seven dollars of his money?"

"Well, yes. But I don't have it now. I meant to pay him back when we got to Tennessee."

The fellow managed to convince the two of them he didn't have any money, and Davy began to feel sorry for him, he looked so pitiful. So Davy and his new friend—who said his name was Henry Myers— went on their way. They traveled together for several days. Davy said he'd never forget Myers' kindness, especially the way Myers told other wagoners about the boy's trouble so that they gave him what money they could spare, up to the amount of three dollars.

"On that money, after Mr. Myers and I had to part, I was able to travel as far as Montgomery Courthouse, in Virginia. I worked there a month for a farmer, ending up with five dollars. Then I worked for a hatter for more than a year. But his business went badly, he broke up, and had to leave the country. I was again penniless and had very few clothes, and they were old ones. I picked up jobs here and there as I could, saved up a little money, and again hit out for home."

This time, Davy was to make it; but there was a while when he was powerfully afraid he wouldn't. This was when he came to Little River.

"The white caps," says Davy, "were flying so that I couldn't get anybody to try to take me across. I argued and argued, but they said any boat going out there was likely to turn over. I told them if I could get a canoe, I'd make a try, caps or no caps. Finding they couldn't persuade me out of it, they agreed I could have a canoe. I tied my clothes to the rope of the canoe so they'd be safe, no matter what happened. Then I put off.

"I'll tell you I found it a mighty ticklish business. When I got right out onto the river, I'd have given the world, if it belonged to me, to have been back on shore. But there wasn't any time to lose now, so I just gritted my teeth and did my best. I turned the canoe across the waves. To do this was bad because the wind was coming from up the river, and I had to turn the canoe in that direction and paddle like fury. My arms ached, and I sweated like a glass pitcher on a muggy hot day, but I kept paddling. I had to go about two miles before I could land, with water slapping up onto me all the way. When I finally came to land, my canoe was about half full of water, and I was wet as a drowned rat. Until I got to a house to warm myself, about three miles from the river, I feared I might drown and freeze at the same time."

A few weeks later Davy got home, without being held up by any more bad luck.

He arrived late in the evening. Several wagons stood in front of the tavern, which looked pretty much unchanged. Davy had grown and filled out so that the family didn't recognize him when he asked to stay overnight. After a while, the family and the wagoners sat down to supper.

They were all eating when Davy noticed his oldest sister, staring at him and frowning.

As they looked at each other she sprang up and, throwing her arms around Davy's neck, she yelled, "Here is my lost brother!"

"I'm sure," says Davy, "I'd never felt before the way I did then. The happiness of my mother and, as a matter of fact, my whole family, made me wish I'd come home and taken a hundred whippings instead of causing them all the worry I had."

Davy found that the family was so glad to see him they forgot all about the whipping his father owed him. This may have been just as well, for he was fifteen years old now, he had his full growth, and he wouldn't have been easy to beat.

4

"FOR TRUE LOVE
A-SARCHIN'"

Y OU CAN TAKE your choice of two stories about
Davy's first sweetheart.

"The first sweetheart he ever had," yarnspinners
said, "was the pride of old Kentucky, Florinda Fury.
She lived up in Gum Hollow, on Goose Creek.
Every winter, she got so plumped up on bear's meat
that when she turned out in the spring, she was
bigger around than a whisky barrel. When a fellow
put his arms around her, it was the same as hugging
a bale of cotton.

"Her two legs were about the roundth of hemlock
trunks, and when she sneezed, it took the leaves
off the trees and scared the setting hens off their
eggs.

"She was just about as pious as a girl of that size
could be—used to set off every Sunday for the
church meeting at Deer Meeting House, carrying
her vittles with her. She always took a rifle, to

55

argue with varmints in case she met them along the trail. And sometimes she carried a rooster in her pocket, in case the parishioners wanted to run a cockfight after service was over.

"There never was a girl that liked anyone the way she did Davy. But she turned against him when he had a few words with her brother. After Davy whopped him, she always talked him down, saying she believed he hadn't acted like a true friend of the family.

"Still and all, in the end she married Ralph Leaf, a fifteenth cousin of Davy's, because she felt it would be an honor to have a relation as famous as Davy was."

Davy's story was rather different.

The way he tells it, he didn't have much truck with girls until he was rather oldish—nearly eighteen. This may have been because he had three sisters, and knew all the tricks and troubles girls went to so as to catch a man or perhaps to keep one.

He'd seen his sisters getting rid of their freckles by rubbing them with honey mixed in buttermilk (a very messy mixture), or rubbing their hides with cucumber pulp to whiten them up. He'd seen them working to soften their lips by putting tallow on them and kissing the middle rail of a five-rail fence. He knew how they cleaned their hair with corn meal to keep it from getting coarse. He'd even caught one of his sisters—the fast one—using cornstarch for face whitening and the red sap from cow-slobber weed to redden her cheeks.

He'd seen them work their tricks to make a man fall in love—sneaking milfoil love potions into a fellow's coffee, and hiding charms such as dry turkey bones or wild turkey gobbler beards under their clothes. He'd seen them make a beau that had fallen out of love fall back in by setting their shoes on the floor at right angles and mumbling poetry, or by tying calico bundles on pawpaw trees with locks of their hair.

All this made him rather skittish, but in time—whether it was because of some of these tricks or not—he had his first tumble into love.

He was working for an honest old Quaker, John Kennedy, who lived about fifteen miles from the Crockett cabin. Davy had worked six months to pay off a note of his father's for forty dollars which Mr. Kennedy held, so during those months he hadn't got a penny for himself. By the time the half-year ended, all his clothes were pretty shabby and some were downright dangerous to wear, especially around women folks. So he'd arranged with Mr. Kennedy to work for some cash money to buy some clothes with; he'd got some new clothes, and soon he thanked his lucky stars he had.

The Quaker's niece, from back in North Carolina, came to pay the Kennedys a visit, and Davy soon found himself head over moccasins in love.

"I've heard people talk about hard loving," says Davy, "but I reckon no poor devil in all this world was ever cursed with such hard love as mine. I thought if all the hills about there were pure gold, and all belonged to me, I'd trade them if I could only talk to her the way I wanted to. But I was afraid to begin, for whenever I'd think of saying anything to her, my heart would start to flutter like a duck in a puddle. And when I tried to outdo the thing and speak out, it would take flight right up into my throat, and choke me like a cold potato.

"Well, it bore on my mind this way till I knew I'd die if I didn't talk to her. So I decided I'd begin and keep trying to speak till, one way or another, my heart would get out of my throat. So one day I went at it, and after several trials I could say a few words. I told her how much I loved her. I said she was the darling object of my soul and body. And then I said I must have her or I'd pine away to nothing, and just die with the consumption."

(For a beginner, this, I think you'll agree, was pretty good. These days, many a man gets married with less pretty talk than this.)

"I found she liked what I was saying to her," Davy goes on. "But she was an honest girl. She told me right off she was engaged to her cousin, a son of the old Quaker.

"This news was worse to me—so I thought at the time—than war, pestilence or famine. But I knew I couldn't do anything about it. I tried to cool off as fast as I could, though since my love was hot enough to bust my boilers, I had hardly enough safety pipes.

"Then I got to wondering what my trouble was," says Davy. "I hit on the idea that it must be my lack of schooling, and was sorry I'd ducked out of Kitchen's school the way I had. I thought I'd try to go to school some."

About a mile and a half from the farm, the Quaker had a married son who was keeping school. Davy went to the son with an idea:

"Suppose," he said, "I go to school four days of the week, and work for you the other two, to pay my board and schooling. Would that be fair?"

The son agreed.

"So," says Davy, "I went at it, learning and working by turns for about six months. I learned to read a little, to write my name, and to cipher to the rule of three. That was all the schooling I was ever to have, though. I broke off the arrangement because I decided I couldn't get along without a wife. So I cut out to hunt one.

"I found a pretty little girl that I'd known since I was very young. But I must have changed or she must have, because I soon got to loving her as bad as I had the Quaker's niece. I got to feeling I'd fight a whole regiment of wildcats if she would say she'd have me. I gave her mighty little peace until she told me, finally, that she would. We fixed the time to be married; and I figured when that day came, I'd be the happiest man in the created world or in the moon or anywhere else.

"Then I was faced with asking her parents, and of course I put that off as long as possible. The wedding day we'd set was on a Thursday, but somehow I didn't manage to get started over to ask them until the Tuesday before."

That morning, when Davy tried to kindle a fire, the thing smoldered and went out—a very bad sign where girls are concerned, as everybody knows. Right off, he took a cocklebur and threw it on his coatsleeve, and instead of sticking, it fell off—another bad sign. Pretty worried by now, he hurried over to the girl's house.

Davy says, "There, I went in and saw her sister. I asked how everybody was. Then I saw from her face something was wrong. She didn't answer as quick as I thought she should, being it was (as I thought) her brother-in-law talking to her. However, I asked her again.

"First thing I knew, she burst into tears. 'My sister,' says she between sobs, 'is going to deceive you. She's marrying another man tomorrow.'

"This was as sudden to me as a clap of thunder on a bright sunshiny day. I thought this was more than any man could stand, and indeed I felt so weak in the knees I thought I'd sink down. I left the house without another word. I concluded I was born for hardships, misery and disappointment. I had no peace day nor night, after that, for several weeks."

As he said, Davy was in a bad way for some time. Then he was able to take a little food, then a little more. Then one day he found he had not only the strength but also the urge to go hunting. He took his rifle and started.

"In spite of my bad time with women," he says, "I found myself stopping in at the house of a Dutch widow and talking to her daughter. The girl was about half as handsome as a stone fence; but she was smart and talkative. She joked at my disappointment, which made me uneasy. Then she started to comfort me, and the way she did this made me more so.

"'Cheer up,' she told me. 'There's as good fish in the sea as ever was caught out of it.'

"I doubted this very much. Moreover, I took this as a hint I could court her—and she was, for a fact, so homely it almost gave me a pain in the eyes to look at her. But I must have been mighty sad-hearted, for I found myself telling her I'd decided the world had been made without a mate for me in it, and I'd never find anyone who'd have me.

"'Oh,' says she, 'don't give up so easy. You come to our reaping. I'll show you one of the prettiest little girls you've ever seen. The girl that fooled you isn't anything to compare to her.'

"'I doubt it,' says I, 'I don't believe it for a minute. She did play a shabby trick on me. I'll never forget her. When's the reaping? I'll be there.'"

The day of the reaping, Davy was on hand, along with a good share of the young men and women from miles around. The men swung their scythes and the girls pulled the flax, until the chores were finished and it was time for the frolic. The men had all fetched something for the supper, which was to come later—some a lick of meal, some a middling of bacon, some a hen, some a possum, some a grab of potatoes or a pocketful of dried apples. There'd been a shooting match a day before, so one young man had brought a quarter of beef.

The frolic began. An old slave was the fiddle-teaser. The men had washed their faces until they shined, and the women were fixed out in their best, from broad-striped homespun to sun-flower calico.

The dancing place was the cabin and the clearing outside with the leaves scraped off it. They'd sprinkled corn bran about on the floor (to help give it a polish) and on the ground (to make dancing easier). The dancing space outside had a circle of big light wood fires around it that flickered red on the dancers and gave each of them a full outfit of short shadows.

Then the dancing was about to start.

"Clear the ring!"

"You, Jake, don't you holler thataway! You sound like a panther."

"Holler? Why I was jest a-whispering. Whoooo-peee! Now I'm beginning to holler!"

"Come here, Suse, and let me pin your dress behind. Your back looks adzactly like a blaze on a white oak!"

"My back's nothing to you, Mister Smarty!"

"Hello, there, fiddler! Give us 'Forked Deer' or we'll give you forked lightnin'!"

"Turn over them rashers o' bacon. They're burnin'."

"Mind your own business, Bob, I've cooked for frolics afore you shed your petticoats."

"Give us 'Leather Britches'! Give us 'Leather Britches'!"

"Oh, shucks, give us 'Rocky Mountain' or 'Misses McCloud.'"

"Oh, I met a frog, with a fiddle and a log, a-askin' of his way to a froooo-lic!"

Soon the fiddler struck up, and if the tune hadn't any words, or nobody knew the words to it, the caller took over. The first tune that night happened to be "Valley Doree," and the caller yelled, in turn, these calls:

Balance all!

Eight hands up, and round you go,
Never git to heaven till you do jest so!

Break and swing and promenade back,
But don't get lost on that back track!

Now you're back,
And now you're slack,
Swing your partners till their necks go crack!

Once and a half and a half all round,
Hollow of your foot knock a hole in the ground!

When you meet your partner, just pat her head,
If she won't eat biscuit, give her bread!

Some likes vittles, some likes beer,
Lead your lady to a rocking cheer.

The girl Davy was to meet was still out primping somewhere, but the Dutch girl trotted up the girl's mother, Mrs. Finley.

"She was no way bashful," says Davy. "She began to praise my red cheeks (which they soon were, with blushing), and she said she had a sweetheart for me. I didn't doubt she'd been told what I came for, and all about it.

"Soon Polly Finley came along. I was plaguy well pleased with her from the word go. She had glossy black hair and dark-blue eyes and a lovely white and pink complexion, like many an Irish girl; but she was the prettiest I'd ever seen.

"After we danced a reel together, I took a seat beside her and we started to talk. I was right glad I'd had all the experience I had, and knew so much about courting, for the words just flowed. I was making as good use of my time as I could, when up came her mother.

"'Well,' says she, joking, 'having a good time, son-in-law.'

"This rather confused me, but I looked on it as a joke of the old lady and tried to pass it off as well as I could. All evening I was careful to pay as much at-

65

tention to her as I could. I went on the old saying of salting the cow to catch the calf."

Davy and Polly left her to join a dance, with the fiddler, and sometimes the dancers, singing the words, and with the caller naming the steps—like this:

I started off from Tennessee,
My old horse wouldn't pull for me.

Now, back step and heel and toe!

He began to fret and slip,
And I began to cuss and whip;
Walk jawbone from Tennessee;
Walk jawbone from Tennessee.

Now, weed corn, cover potaters, and double shuffle!

I fed my horse in the poplar trough.
It made him catch the whooping cough.
My old horse died in Tennessee,
And willed his jawbone here to me.
Walk jawbone from Tennessee;
Walk jawbone from Tennessee.

About midnight, the Dutch widow sang out, "Stop that dancing and come get your supper!"

Supper was set in the yard on a table made of forks stuck in the ground and a plank from the stable loft, with sheets for tablecloths.

While the company took seats, the widow told them, "Knives is scarce, so give what there is to the girls and let the balance use their hands; they was invented before knives, anyhow. Now just walk into the fat of this land."

They danced until near day, and then played some games. One, "Mister Boatlander," was a kissing game. A couple stepped up to Davy and sang,

Mister Boatlander, 'tis time we were marchin'—
Marchin' around for true love a-sarchin'.
Call your true love, call her now or never.
Call her true name, and tell you how you love her.

Davy sang out, "Polly Finley!" Polly stepped up, blushing and smiling, her blue eyes sparkling. Then everybody sang:

Miss Polly Finley, this child says he loves you—
Nothin' in the world he loves like he likes you.
His heart you've gained, his hand he'll give you.
One sweet kiss, and sorry for to leave you.

67

Polly tilted back her head, and Davy kissed her red lips.

"I began to think," says Davy, "that the Dutch girl had told me the truth when she said there were still good fish in the sea.

"As soon as I could I went to see Polly, and also to find out what sort of people they were at home," says Davy. "I found her father a very clever man, and her mother as full of talk as ever. She seemed to want to find out all about me, to see how I'd do for her girl. I couldn't catch sight of Polly anywhere, and I was on needles and pins to know where she was.

"Soon, though, she came home from a meeting. There was a young man with her. He seemed to be setting up claim to her. Matter of fact, he chattered so that I couldn't hardly slip a word in edgeways. I began to wonder if I was barking up the wrong tree again; but I made up my mind to stand up to my rack, fodder or no fodder. To know her mind a little, I began to talk about starting home.

"'Well,' says I, 'it's near night, and I've got fifteen miles to go home.'

"'Oh,' says she, 'must you go? Mr. Smith is just leaving. Where is Mr. Smith's hat, now?'

"Well, thinks I to myself, that shows which way the wind blows. But the fellow couldn't take a hint,

68

and she came over to my side of the room and sat with me. When she said very hearty that I mustn't go that long way home at night, I could see she preferred me all hollow.

"I commenced a close courtship, while he sat by himself, looking like a poor man at a country frolic. Every once in a while, I looked at him fierce as a wildcat. At last he left and I stayed a-courting until Monday morning, and then cut for home."

A few more meetings, and some more courting, and then Davy felt sure he was right and went ahead and popped the question.

"She was agreeable," says Davy, "and we set the day for the wedding. I made arrangements for the in-fare (a big frolic we had in Tennessee two or three days after that wedding) at my father's house. Then it was time for me to ask her parents for her.

"Her father liked me and said yes right off, but her mother was mighty wrathy. Say what I could, I couldn't get her to agree. Well, I decided that all I wanted was to have Polly on my side. I knew she was then, but I couldn't tell how soon some other fellow might knock my nose out of joint again.

"'Polly, I'll come next Thursday,' I said, 'and bring a saddled horse for you. You be ready to go.'

"Well, as it happened, by Thursday old Mr. Finley had convinced his wife she should accept me for

69

a son-in-law. She begged my pardon handsomely, and we had the wedding at the Finleys' home. What's more, she gave us two likely cows and calves as a marriage-portion, and had a gay time of it at the wedding frolic and at the infare, too."

Davy figured that now he was married, he didn't need anything more in the whole world. Soon, though, he found he couldn't have made a bigger mistake. Now that he had a wife he needed everything else. He rented a small farm and cabin, and went to work. He and Polly were able to buy what they wanted for the house, thanks pretty much to a present of fifteen whole dollars from his old friend the Quaker. Polly was good at weaving, and that helped.

They worked along for several years, but renting a farm came high and, as Davy put it, "I found it wasn't what it was cracked up to be. In this time we had two sons. I found I was better at increasing my family than my fortune. I decided to hunt a better place to get along; and as I knew I'd better do it before my family go too big, so I'd have less to carry.

"The Duck and Elk river country was just beginning to settle, and I decided to try that. I found it a very rich country, and so new that game of many sorts was very plentiful. As I remember it, I lived here in the years 1809 and 1810, and then I moved to Franklin county and settled on Bean Creek. I stayed there for some years."

As luck will have it, the people who knew Davy in those days have given us some information about his marriage and his life in the new settlement that for some reason or other Davy left out. Here's what they add:

"Davy's wife was a streak of lightning set up edgeways and buttered with quicksilver. She could blow out the moonlight and sing a wolf to sleep. The children were what you'd expect: they could outrun, outjump, and outscream almost any creature in creation. They could also outfight a middling-sized thunderstorm.

"When the family moved, they piled all their bedding and furniture and cooking things into a wagon, and started to travel. All day they'd plod along through the trees, and when the road was bumpy or went uphill, they'd pile out and walk for a while. When the road was boggy, Davy'd chop down or pull up some young saplings and fill holes with them so the wheels could roll across. Some days out, Davy couldn't tell for the life of him whether there was supposed to be a trail or not, except by noticing the blazes chopped on the trees. At night, they'd sleep under the stars.

"So it went till they came to a stopping place at the head of the Mulberry fork of the Elk River, not far from the River Duck.

"When a family moved into a new place back then, they usually had one party after another. They did this so they could get people from around about to come and do all the work.

"'There doesn't seem to be a cabin in this clearing,' they'd say. 'In fact, there doesn't seem to be any clearing. So let's have some parties, and make a clearing and raise a cabin, just to pass the time. P.S. Bring some food along, will you?'

"The first day, the choppers would fell the trees and cut them to the right lengths; the teamsters would haul them to the place where they were to be used; the carpenters would split the clapboards and the puncheons; and then everybody would put down the foundation.

"The second day would be the day of the house-raising, with everybody asked to pitch in, put down the floors, pile up the logs, make the chimney, and cut the doors and windows.

"It got so that the minute people saw a covered wagon, with a family and furniture piled up in it, moving into the neighborhood, their bones would begin to ache.

"Of course, Davy Crockett, with all his strength,

didn't need any help with the clearing of the land or with the building of his cabin or furniture—any help, that is, that his wife and the children couldn't give him. This was lucky, since there wasn't anyone in this new country to help anyhow.

"But the family had a ripsnorting frolic for itself at the housewarming. Music was 'pervided,' as they say, by a wolf and a panther.

"The soil on the Mulberry fork was even richer than the soil on the Nolachucky. If you planted potatoes there, you soon had a mountain on your hands out in the vegetable garden. Pumpkin vines grew so fast that they wore out some of the pumpkins just dragging them along the ground. Even when pumpkins didn't wear out but slid along nice and easy across the soft soil, when Davy went out to pick one he had to run like a shooting star scared by an earthquake to catch up with it.

"There was work a-plenty. Chasing pumpkins was just the start of it. You had to break the bad habit that squirrels and raccoons had of eating the corn off of all the ears and you had to discourage the liking wolves, panthers and bears had for sheep and hogs. And even when the animals weren't pestering Davy, falling trees had a way of knocking holes in the worm fences so that the cattle would get into the wrong fields. Well, Davy or someone had to chase the cattle into the right fields and repair the fences.

"Davy's wife had to grind meal in the hand-mill, churn butter, make linsey cloth out of flax and wool, tan leather, sew up moccasins and hunting shirts, cook the mess and help make crops.

"The children had to do any chores left over.

"So Davy had to think up useful ways to speed the work. He planted corn, for instance, by shooting it into crevices with a shotgun, and he planted it nice and even that way, too. He figured out a way to harness a hurricane so it would turn a spinning wheel or work the hand-mill. He also tamed animals and taught them to do this and that little thing around the place to help out the family.

"He tamed a wolf so that if anyone in the family was cold, this wolf would shiver for them.

"A panther that Davy tamed was also very useful. When Davy'd come home late of an inky night, the panther would light the way to bed with the fire in his eyes. He'd brush the hearth off every morning with this tail, and Saturdays, he'd do Mrs. Crockett's heavy work. He raked in all her garden seed with his claws and helped to curry-comb the horses with his nails.

"Davy often said that the smartest animal the family ever had was a bear his little girl, Pinette, met in

74

the woods one day when she was out for a walk. The bear used to follow Pinette to church, waddling along behind her and carrying her pocketbook, with the money for the collection, in his mouth. At last this bear got so tame that it would come into the house to warm itself and meet the family.

"From the start, the bear thought well of Davy, and Davy thought very well of the bear.

"Davy named the bear Death Hug and taught him how to smoke a pipe. While the bear sat in one corner smoking, Davy sat in the other with his pipe. They couldn't talk to each other, but they would look, and Davy always knew by the shine in Death Hug's eyes what he wanted to say.

"Death Hug would sit up nights when his master was out late, and would open the door when Davy came home. Then, with the panther to light the way to the bedroom, it would be a pleasure for Davy to go to bed—even if the night was black as a bear's cave, as it often was, of course, in the midst of the forest trees.

"Death Hug, though, was the greatest at churning butter—did all the churning for the family in less time than it'd take a streak of lightning to run around a sweet-potato patch, and a little patch, at that.

"One time when Davy had a race with a steam-

Davy's Pet Bear, Death Hug
1850 Almanack

boat, Death Hug was a big help to him. The two of them walked out to the woods together and cut down a hollow tree. They cut open one side, corked up both ends, whittled a pair of paddles, and launched their boat on the brown Mississippi, just as a sidewheel steamboat came chugging along.

"Davy paddled the boat. Death Hug sat in the stern, holding the American flag in his paw, smoking his pipe and steering the boat with his tail, which he dangled in the water for a rudder.

"They left the steamboat so far behind that the thing just quit trying. And that was smart, because if the boat had put on any more steam, it would have blown up its boilers."

ON THE WARPATH

T HE STORY THAT fireside yarnspinners or fellows who wrote spread around about Davy's part in the war with the Indians made the whole thing sound easy as falling off a small log for him. Here's the way it went:

"An Indian chief—a Shawanoe from the Miami Valley named Tecumseh—started the trouble in the war back there where Davy showed what an Indian fighter he was.

"This Tecumseh was almost as fine a hunter as Davy was. Once, when the Indians had a hunting match to see who was the best hunter in the tribe of the Shawanoes, Tecumseh brought in thirty deerskins in the day and the night of the match. The best the next man to him could fetch was twelve.

"Tecumseh was also a great chief. If he could get enough Indians together and stand up on something and wave his arms around and make a speech to them, he could get them onto the warpath, tomahawks, bows and arrows and all, quicker than a buck could jump a thicket.

"It seems that this year he went one place after another and told thousands of Indians what he wanted them to do.

"He visited the Seminoles. These Indians lived in Florida and wore clothes with green and yellow and blue stripes. They'd killed off most of the Euchees and had married up with the rest of them, so you can see they were pretty fierce.

"Then Tecumseh went and talked to the Creeks and the Cherokees. These Indians lived along all the creeks in Georgia, Alabama and north Florida, so there were a good many of them. Most of them spoke the Muskhogean language, which doubtless must have given them bad tempers. They had White Towns to have their peace meetings in, and Red Towns to have their war meetings in.

"Tecumseh said, 'Let's have our meeting in a Red Town this time.'

"Finally, he went to make a speech to the Des Moins, in Missouri. These fellows were great trappers—made quite a fine living for themselves by selling pelts of bear, beaver, otter, raccoon and squirrel. But they were fierce warriors, too. And with their hair shaved off all except a strip down the middle that looked like a crest, they looked fierce. Nobody liked this except the Des Moins Indians, and that suited them fine.

"Visiting all these tribes, Tecumseh made his speech. He told them to put on their war paint right away and start out on the warpath. He was a great speaker, and soon they were following his advice.

"When news about this got to Davy, he made sure he was right and then went ahead. 'The harvest's in,' he said, 'all but two or three mountains of potatoes, and the children and the panther can finish them up. And I can get back in time for spring planting if I scoot.' So he asked to be excused for a while, and went off to fight the Indians.

"He joined up with Colonel Coffee's army, just when news came that the red men were marching in that direction. 'That's right thoughtful,' says Davy. 'Comes in handy. But we won't be outdid in politeness by any Indians. We'll march in *their* direction.'

"So the army started marching at a breakneck speed, covering six whole miles an hour, about the fastest an army ever did march.

"Davy went on ahead, to be a scout and smell out what the Indians' plans were. He scouted among all the tribes, and then hurried back to camp just when Colonel Coffee and his men had decided to call it a day and rest for the night. The army was plumb fagged out.

"'Take it easy,' Davy told them. Then he cooked up a mess of bear he'd killed along the way, served it for dinner, and then hoisted a pup tent for every man in that brave army. Just before the men went to bed, Davy told them what he'd learned. Then, while the army slept, Davy washed the dishes, kept watch, and got things ready for the morning.

"The next day, the fighting was pretty fierce. The Indians were all painted up, of course. What's more, they whooped and yelled, and the Creeks and Cherokees did it in the Muskhogean language. And the whole lot did whatever fierce things they could think up.

"But Davy grinned, which was about as hard on Indians as it was on coons. What's more, he yelled so loud that anybody that wanted to couldn't tell about his voice, but had to paint a picture of it. And yelling like that, and banging away with old Betsy until smoke blotted out the sunshine, Davy fought the Indians on the Coosa River, the Tennessee River, and the Talapoosa River. Then he fought them on the smaller streams.

"This went on for weeks, and became most tiresome.

"Then, when Davy'd run out of rivers and

streams, and the Indians had run out of the country, Davy went back home. He got there in time for the spring planting, of course. Davy Crockett always kept all his promises, whether he'd made them or not."

Well, there are a few facts in this story that aren't exactly true. The whole thing wasn't anything like that easy. From start to finish, the war was pretty grim.

Tecumseh, true enough, made fiery speeches and managed to fill the tribes he talked to as full of zeal as he was. And he won to his side Indians all the way from the Gulf to Canada: that's history. And the War with England led him to think that the year 1813 was a fine time to strike.

In August, the frontier people around Lake Tensaw, in the southern part of what later came to be Alabama, heard the Indians were on the warpath. Many left their crops standing and their houses open to anyone that wanted to plunder them. They all rushed to the stockade that old man Mims had built against a time of just such trouble. Some volunteers came hurrying up from New Orleans to help defend the place, and they built more stockades inside the old ones.

All this didn't do much good against the forces that Tecumseh and his friends got together. On August 29, a thousand Indians, led by a half-breed named Bill Weatherford (his Indian name was Red Eagle), attacked the stockades, set them afire with flaming arrows, and massacred four hundred men, women and children.

General Andrew Jackson was lying abed in his big house, the Hermitage, near Nashville. He'd been badly wounded in a duel a while back. But when he heard what had happened, he sent spies out among the Indians—half-breeds and frontiersmen who knew the woods. He had messengers go to see the Creeks most likely to side with the settlers—also to see the Choctaws and th Cherokees. This way he had hopes it would be possible to find out what the warring Indians were up to. And when the legislature passed a bill to raise thirty-five hundred militiamen, the General had his left arm trussed up in a sling, got himself hoisted up on a horse and started off.

Davy heard, too, and acted as you'd expect.

"Don't go, Davy." Polly begged him when she saw him getting ready. "I'm a stranger in these parts. I don't have any relations nearby. The children and I'll be left in a lonesome and dangerous way."

"Well," Davy said, "It's mighty hard to go against such arguments. But if every man waited till his wife was willing for him to go to war, there'd be no fighting done. Soon the Indians would be here, too, and we'd all be killed in our houses."

So Davy went to Winchester, where the militia was being mustered. Soon he and more than a thousand riflemen were moving across country, wearing the coonskin caps, the fringed hunting shirts and the leather britches they wore for hunting.

"I never could forget those times, even if I tried," says Davy. "They were at least fair-to-middling interesting, I thought.

"One thing I found was that some very tough times in a war came when there wasn't any battle going on. For instance, I remember one of the hardest nights I ever went through—and it had nothing to do with a battle, the hardness of it, I mean.

"It started when Major Gibson in his fine uniform came riding into camp on his fine horse and asked my captain to name some of his best huntsmen and rifle shots to join a scouting party.

"Captain pointed at me and said, 'This is the best hunter and the best shot, too, in Tennessee, and he'll go as far as any man.' (Of course, he was in a hurry, and didn't have time to cover all my good points.)

"Thirteen of us (a most uneasy number) went deep into Indian territory, thinking every minute, of course, we'd be ambushed or surrounded. After a time, we took two trails, with Major leading seven of the scouts and me the rest. We planned to meet at a certain crossroads at nightfall, and compare what we'd found out. Soon my party met a half-breed named Jack Thompson. He wore a deer tail in his hair—the sign General Jackson had thought up—so we asked him to join us and guide us in the strange country.

"'Not in daylight, I won't,' says he. 'Too dangerous. I'll meet you tonight.'

"So I fixed it for us to meet at those crossroads; and he was to let us know he was there by hollering like an owl.

"That night we spent waiting, and waiting, and waiting. The hours dragged on and on, it seemed to the day of doom. The moon came up, and we knew from its height that eight o'clock came, then nine, then ten. The longer time went, the more rustlings and scary little noises we heard, and the more ideas we got about what had gone wrong. We thought of many ways Major Gibson and his men had got killed. We managed to remember a dozen things Thompson had said or done that showed us he was for the enemy and meant to betray our hiding place. We whispered about our worries.

"A mite past ten o'clock, I heard an owl call. I had to decide whether I'd answer or not. If my answer brought a tribe of Indians down on us, I felt fairly sure I'd be regretful. On the other hand, we needed Jack's help, if he was on our side. At last I made up my mind, answered the call (a bit hoarsely, I guess), and then heard my heart thump like an Indian drum while we waited and waited some more. About a thousand years later, the sounds told us Thompson was coming alone, and that was a relief, I'll swear.

"But it turned out we'd just started to wait, because Major's party still hadn't come. The autumn frost chilled us deep down to our bones, but of course we couldn't move to brisk up our blood, nor could we kindle a fire. The moon kept going its slow way across the sky, and again there were thousands of sounds that had to be listened to and worried about. After another eternity or two, there were streaks of light and then it was morning. There still weren't signs of Major; but we could move. We were so on edge and played out with worrying that it would have been a relief to march down the throat of a crocodile. We pushed on."

The next night, it so happened, they got the news about Indian movements. They rode all through the moonlit night to report to camp, and soon after they arrived, Major Gibson's party came in with the same news.

"What stuck in my mind," says Davy, "was

this—the all-night ride was hard, of course, coming after about thirty-six hours without sleep, when we're dead tired. But it wasn't near so hard as waiting and waiting, when you couldn't do another thing."

Another hard part of that war was unexpected, too—the starving, and that was something else Davy never forgot in all his born days.

A good share of the time, General Jackson had under him twenty-five hundred men. Some, like Davy, were mounted; so there were thirteen hundred horses, too. A body like this needed ten wagonloads of provisions every single day. To get through a week, they needed a thousand bushels of grain, twenty tons of meat, a thousand gallons of whiskey and tons of other stuff.

But they didn't have these—not by a long shot— in that war. Contractors were supposed to bring in the food, sure: the General had arranged it before he left Nashville. But they found it sinful hard to get into the forests with all the food that was needed, or anything like it, or, as a matter of fact, any food at all. Any place this army camped, the countryside would yield game for a while; but soon there wouldn't be any varmints left to shoot. And the army would go on half rations for weeks running.

There were times when the men had to get along

on nothing but acorns, and these made pretty poor eating, as anyone knows who's ever tried them.

Davy and the best of the hunters in the outfit were sent out regularly to knock down all the game in sight and bring it back to camp.

He tells of one time when a detachment he was with had hunger gnawing at them for more days than were comfortable.

"We went on," he says, "killing nothing to eat till, at last, we all were about ready to give up the ghost and lie down and die. We came to a prairie that looked promising. At last I found a squirrel, which I wouldn't have drawn a bead on at home. I shot him, but he got into a hole in a tree. He was small game, but in a fix like that, a man's not as choosy as usual. I climbed the tree, thirty feet high and without a limb, and pulled him out by the heels.

"I soon killed two other squirrels. Then by great luck, I found some turkeys and killed one. I went back to camp, and we started to cook some of our game, though we had neither salt nor bread. Just at this moment, we saw some of our men who'd got provisions down the creek, coming toward us. They had some flour, they told us. We measured out a cupful to each. With this, we thickened our soup, when our turkey was cooked. Credit this or not, as you choose, but I'll swear I enjoyed that meal about as much as any I ever had."

All through that war, it was likely that the men time after time would be famished for food. And famine was hard to take for men who'd lived on the fat of the land, as the saying went, before they went to war.

The shooting part of the war could be tough, too, Davy found.

It was tough, for instance, at Talladega, a Creek town that had declared for Jackson. On November 7, an Indian wearing a deer tail in his scalp lock came running to Jackson's camp, where Davy was. His town, he said, thirty miles south, had been surrounded by Red Eagle's braves. His people were low on food and almost out of water. This Indian runner had covered himself with the hide of a hog, got out of the fort on all fours, and rooted and grunted his way through the enemy lines.

"In an hour," says Davy, "we were marching. Soon after sunrise, near the fort at Talladega, our lines made a hollow square. We sent old Major Russell, with his spy company, and Captain Evans's company, to bring on the battle. From the ramparts of the fort, the Indians were waving and hollering. Russell couldn't think what they meant, so he waved back in a good-natured way. Of a sudden, the fort doors flew open and two ran out, naked as the day they were born except for a great deal of paint. They grabbed Russell's horse by the bridle and shouted and waved. It wasn't treachery, as at first seemed likely. They were pointing at a nearby creek, with trees along the banks, trying (as it turned out) to get him to understand that the enemy was hid behind the trees and the bank.

"They'd stopped our men just in the nick of time. The hidden Red Sticks (as the enemy were called) fired a volley. Then they came rushing like a cloud of Egyptian locusts, and screaming like banshees. Russell's company flipped off their horses and scurried into the fort. The horses wheeled and ran for our line, with the Indians hot behind. We saw these Indians were naked, too, and painted as red as Kentucky cardinals.

"Again there was a bad time for waiting—waiting till the enemy was close enough before shooting. When we fired, a few came on and grappled, but most broke like a herd of stampeded steers. But they soon got near to the other line, where another volley was fired. So we kept them running from one line to another, always under fire.

"But remember, we were under fire, too—with arrows whizzing by us (if we were lucky) and bullets coming our way, too. Some may get over the shock of seeing the man next to them shot down in a battle. I suppose some may get so they don't wonder if the next bullet may have their address on it. Well, I never did. That made it pesky hard to stand, I don't mind confessing.

"At last there was a break in our line through which many got away. But we killed well above three hundred of them and wounded others. We lost fifteen of our men, as brave fellows as ever lived or died. We buried them all in one grave, and said prayers over it. Then we trompled the ground and burned fires over the grave and other ground around it, so the enemy couldn't find the grave and scalp our dead.

"After a parley with the Indians in the fort, we headed back to our camp. Before we got there, two more men died of wounds."

Tough as this fight at Talladega was, another was even tougher. From Fort Williams, Davy went with General Jackson's army toward the Horseshoe bend of the Talapoosa River.

Not far from the bend, they came on Indian signs a-plenty, so it seemed a good idea to set up camp for the night in a well-protected place. Two hours before sunup, the troops were jarred from sleep by shots fired by the guards. The men leaped up, threw fuel on the fires, and fell back. They formed a hollow square in the dark.

"We'd hoped," Davy explains, "that the Red Sticks would come in and when they were lighted up by our own fires, we would shoot from the dark. But they fooled us. What they did was sneak around on our flanks and fire on us in the dark. We shot back, taking our aim at the rifle flashes. This lasted all night. In the morning, they'd gone, leaving four of our men dead."

Davy and others made horse litters for the wounded, then began a retreat. Soon they came to a wide creek and started to cross it. At a most awkward time, when half the men were across and others were splashing in the cold water, the Indians began flipping bullets at their left wing. Then a force of Indians came up on the rear, where the artillery men were. The bad part was that the artillery men had poor cover, while the Indians shot from behind some big logs.

This wasn't as bad as it seemed, though, because General Jackson, wise old fox that he was, had foreseen things might go just this way. He'd made a plan—that the rear was to hold the Red Sticks long enough for two flank columns to recross the creek above and below, to circle the Indians, and then to close in. The idea was to get the Red Sticks into much the same fix they'd got into at Talladega. This movement was started.

93

But at that worst of times, two cowardly officers crossed the creek out of reach of the fire, leaving their men leaderless. The right and left columns began to give way. Then the center column began to give way, too.

"We were in an awful mess," says Davy. "You see, part of our men were on one side of the creek, and part on the other. The Indians were pouring in on us, as hot as fresh mustard to a sore shin. I think General Jackson's men came nearer being whipped right then than they were at any other time. Being one of them, I couldn't help but be interested."

William Carroll, so Davy always claimed, saved the day "by greater bravery than I ever saw any other man show." He rallied twenty-five men, Davy among them, around him, and led them right ahead through a regular storm of bullets. John Coffee, who'd been wounded, rolled off one of the litters and, though he was in terrible pain, led a company to Carroll's side. The men led by Carroll managed to divide the Indians and then to force them back to the hills, in spite of very bad losses. That was the end of this engagement, and a most lucky one, too.

The battle was the end of the war for Davy, as it happened. "My horse had got crippled;" he said, "and was unfit for service. As some enforcements had come up, I thought they'd be able to get along without me. I got a furlough and went home."

That same month, while Davy was still on furlough, General Jackson and his army won over a huge band of Indians in the battle of Horseshoe Bend on the Talapoosa. It broke the back of the Red Stick war. Soon after, the great chiefs, including Red Eagle, surrendered.

6

SQUIRE, COLONEL AND CONGRESSMAN

BACK FROM THE WARS, Davy worked his farm and hunted, just the way he had before. He was happy as a lark to be back with the family again.

Then the world suddenly turned black for him. Polly became sick. He watched her suffering with a helplessness that was hard for even so strong a man to bear. A few months later, she died, leaving him and the three children—one a baby—very lonely. "This," he said, "is the hardest trial that ever falls to the lot of man."

He couldn't bear the idea of scattering the children, so he got his youngest brother and his family to come live with him. They did their best for the children, but as the months went by, Davy couldn't feel that they took the place of a mother.

After some time, he got to know a widow, Elizabeth Patton, who had a little boy and a little girl of her own.

"I began to think," says Davy, "we could do something for each other, maybe."

When he talked with her, he found Elizabeth had the same thought, and they agreed to marry. They had a good life together, giving Davy's children and Elizabeth's children a good upbringing and, as Davy put it, "raising a fine crop of children of our own."

Not long after the wedding, however, Elizabeth had a bad fright. Davy was away exploring a part of the frontier that was opening for settlement. He didn't return as soon as had been planned, and news came that he had died. Fact was, he'd had an attack of malaria that prevented his coming home for a time. When at last he got home, Elizabeth was astonished and of course delighted.

A year after their marriage, feeling they might do better in a new home, they moved about eighty miles onto some land newly bought from the Chickasaw Indians. This was on Shoal Creek. And it was there that Davy Crockett got into government.

"We stayed there two or three years," says he, "without any government at all, and nobody missing it. Then so many people flocked in that didn't care about other people's rights we figured we'd better set up a government. We didn't know much about how this was done, so we probably did it wrong. We didn't fix any laws, you see. All we did was appoint magistrates and constables and such to keep order."

Neighbors figured that it stood to reason that since Davy was a great Indian fighter and a great hunter, he should be a magistrate, so they made him one. Magistrate Crockett worked without fuss or feathers. When a man wouldn't pay a debt, the constable would arrest him and bring him up for trial. Davy would scare the debt out of him. If someone was charged with earmarking his neighbor's hogs, or with stealing something, Davy would have him brought in by the constable, then he'd try and have him punished.

"We kept this up," says Davy, "till the Tennessee legislature brought us into Giles county and made all us magistrates squires by law. I had a hard time now because instead of just telling the constable what to do, I had to write out things called warrants—had to write out my findings, too. Since I could barely scribble out my own name, and since I'd never read a law book in my life, this was a huckleberry above my persimmon. But I studied, improved my handwriting, and finally got so I could write warrants as pretty as you please and keep my record book to boot.

"I'm right proud to say my judgments were never appealed from, and if they had been, by grannies, they'd have stuck like wax. Reason was, I based them on common justice and honesty between man and man, and I depended on natural born sense and not on law-learning to guide me."

Well, being in government often is a hard habit to break, and it was for Davy. Next thing he knew, he was elected a colonel in the militia, which was why he was called Colonel Crockett the rest of his life. A while after, in 1821, he was put up for the state legislature.

At first, in some ways, being a candidate proved to be harder for him than the waiting or the starving or even the shooting in the Creek War had been. Now he had to make speeches and, says he, "The mere thought of making a speech made my knees mighty weak and set my heart fluttering almost as bad as that Quaker girl did when I first fell in love long before. Somehow, my buckskin collar got fearfully tight and choked me as much as it'd choke Jonah to swallow the whale."

He worked up to it step by step. At first, at meetings, he'd wait till everybody else had orated and the crowd was dead tired; then he'd step up and treat the crowd.

"The way Colonel Crockett electioneers," some of the neighbors said, "he and his boys hunt until twelve o'clock every night. They get heaps of coonskins and trade 'em for whisky at the rate of two for a quart. Then he puts on a buckskin hunting shirt with two big pockets in it. He puts a bottle in one and a twist of chewing tobacco in t'other, and starts out. When he meets a voter, he pulls out the bottle and gives him a drink. The fellow will be sure, before he drinks, to throw away his quid of tobacco. So when the man's finished, the colonel pulls his twist out of his pocket and gives him a chaw. Crockett never leaves a man worse off than he found him—and you can't say that about many politicians, you know."

His next way of campaigning was a smidgeon more complicated. He not only treated; he also told jokes and talked with people. The neighbors—and Davy, too—liked to tell a story about a time when he had to think fast to manage to treat, to joke and to talk. It seems that at the Cross Roads near Shoal Creek a gander-shanked Yankee, Job Snelling, had set up a shop to serve the crowd at an election meeting. Job came from a cheating family. His father had invented wooden nutmegs and his mother oak pumpkin seeds. He himself had thought up the idea of selling mahogany sawdust for cayenne pepper at a fine profit. Well, Job was always bragging he was wide awake—said he even slept with one eye half open and the other half shut. So he said anyone that could get the better of him was free to do so.

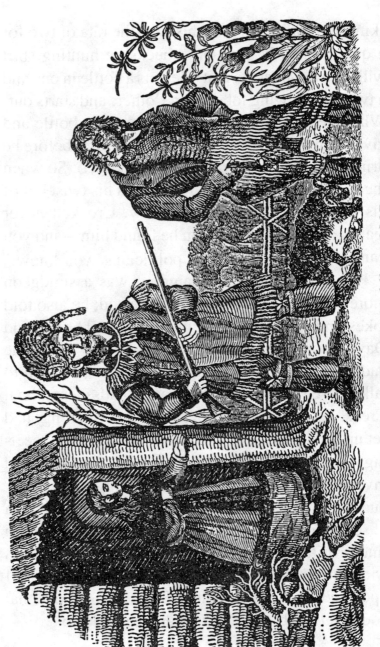

Davy Confronts a Yankee Peddler—1837 Almanack

Davy came along to the meeting without a cent, and was at once asked to treat. He led the crowd to Job's store and ordered a horn for everyone. But Job pointed at a sign he'd painted—PAY TODAY AND TRUST TOMORROW. Davy had to confess he couldn't pay, and the crowd vanished about as quick as a scared fox does. It was plain he had to treat or he'd lose the election sure as there were snakes in Virginia. So Davy rushed out into the forest, shot a coon, skinned it, and came back to the store with the skin. Most of the voters followed him. He traded the skin for a treat—the way people did in those parts where coonskins were the same as money—and everyone had a treat. He told a few stories to get the crowd in a good humor, and started to ask for votes, when the crowd asked for another treat.

He looked up, and the dratted sign was still there. It looked as if he'd have to shoot another coon. Then he looked down. Job had flung the skin under the counter, and one end was sticking out between the logs. He gave it a jerk, and it followed his hand as well as if he'd been the owner. Davy slammed it on the counter, and Job delivered the treats. Davy talked to the voters some more, and then was asked to treat again.

He looked down right away this time, and was happy to see the skin was sticking out as before.

Well, this was the way things went for some while. Ten times Davy used that skin to buy treats, and from a fellow, too, that was known to be as sharp as a steel trap. The crowd not only went for the treats; when they heard the story of how Davy had outdone Job (for the story spread like smoke on a windy day), they decided a man that smart should have their votes.

From giving treats, telling jokes and talking, Davy worked up to making short speeches, like this one:

"Gentlemen, I don't want you to think I've come electioneering. I just crept out of the cane to see what discoveries I can make among the white folks. They tell me I've been put up for the legislature. All I can say is, if I'm elected, I'll do the best I can. I've killed two wolves and got a bounty of three dollars for each scalp. So I'm ready to treat everybody to a horn."

He was elected with double the votes of the man against him and nine to spare. In the legislature he soon learned a good deal about government and served his district well.

There's proof of this: Soon after he was elected and had gone to the state capitol, bad news came from home. A heavy freshet had swept away a grist mill, a powder mill, and a distillery he'd built, leaving him much in debt. When he'd paid up as best he could, he was without a penny. The best thing seemed to be to move and try a new start. So he and Elizabeth and the children, they moved to the westmost part of the state, near where the Obion River joins the Mississippi. And though he was new to those parts, the next election he was elected to the legislature by his neighbors. They'd heard about him, you see, and were sure he'd do.

Next thing Davy knew, his neighbors asked him to run for the United States Congress.

"No," he told them, "that's a big step above my knowledge. I don't know a thing about Congress matters."

He was forced to run anyhow. But it looks as if too many people agreed with him, because he lost. Still and all, it was only by two votes, so when the next election came in 1827, he decided to try again. By now, he'd learned to make first-rate speeches, and long ones at that. So, often he'd have meetings of his own to make speeches at.

In a town where there was a meeting, people knew when and where to go by watching for the blue smoke that curled out of the long barbecue pits in the grove. There they'd find pigs, shoats, lambs and veal on the spits, smoking and getting brown, and smelling wonderful. They'd also find more people lined up to watch the parade. Part of the parade would be militia companies in their marching suits, their brass buttons shining to put your eyes out and the plumes bobbing on their hats. Ahead of them would be fellows playing fifes and drums. After the militia would come the volunteer firemen, the Temperance Cadets and any other groups that had uniforms. If the town was lucky, it might rustle up a float or two—wagons decorated up, you know, with flowers, flags, and signs.

The people would cheer, and the horses and mules would get scared and would try to break their tethers. Sometimes they'd do it, too.

After the animals had got caught and tied up again, and the parade had ended, there'd be the feast. Everybody would sit at the long tables cover-ed with white sheets or red checkered tablecloths.

Then Candidate Crockett would climb up on a stand, take off his coonskin cap and buckskin coat, and make his speech. The ladies kept cool, if they could, by waving turkey tail fans, and the men took their minds off the heat by whittling sticks.

"I was running," says Davy, "against two clever men, Colonel Alexander and General Arnold, taken together a pretty considerable load for any one man to carry. Being I was from the backwoods, they seemed to take me as pretty much of a joke. So they didn't so much as mention me. They were working against each other, while I was going ahead for myself, and mixing among the people the best I could. I found the sign was good, almost everywhere I went.

"At one place, it happened we all had to make a speech, and it fell on me to start. I went by the old saying, 'A short horse is soon curried,' and didn't speak long. Colonel Alexander came next, then General Arnold. The general took pains to answer Arnold, but didn't even let on I was running. He'd talked for some time when a flock of guinea fowls came along and made the sort of loud chattering those noisy little brutes can make. They confused him so that he stopped and asked that they be shooed away.

"I let him finish, then walked up to him and said quite loud, 'Well, colonel, you're the first man I ever saw that understood the language of fowls. You weren't good enough to name me in your speech. Then when my little friends came up and began to holler, 'Crockett, Crockett, Crockett,' you went and had to stop and drive them away.' This raised a shout among the people for me."

Now, just to show how a story sometimes grows, let me set down the way some writer told about the election:

"It struck the insects, birds and animals of the district that it'd be handy to have Davy (and his rifle, old Betsy) away off in Washington, D.C., where he couldn't hunt. So they worked for his election. The crickets chirped 'Cr-k-tt.' The guinea hens clucked 'Cr-cr-kt.' The bullfrogs chunked 'Cro-o-ck-ett.' The wild animals growled 'Gr-r-ro-gett.' And the Crockett family's pet animals, who'd had better schooling, showed their white teeth and hollered '*Crockett forever*,' just as plain. Sounded as if they were all voting for him. So their votes were counted, along with the people's, and he was elected by a vote that was unanimous and 307 votes over. This was enough to send him to Congress not once but twice."

I don't mind pointing out two things, at least, that are wrong with this: (1) his election wasn't unanimous: he won by 2,748 votes; (2) he wasn't elected in one try to serve two terms: he had to run again in 1829, which he did, winning this time by 202 votes.

The story people told about Davy's first trip to Washington may have another mistake or two in it. It goes this way:

Before starting, Congressman Crockett heard that people there were great dancers. So he taught Death Hug and his brand-new pet alligator, Old Mississippi, to do all the latest dances. The Honorable Davy and Death Hug and Old Mississippi and a fiddler would go to a forest opening. While the fiddler played "Grind the Bottle," "The Frog and the

Mouse" or "The Crow and the Tailor," Davy taught his pets to dance.

Then Congressman Crockett and his pets hugged everybody in the family, including all the animals, and they all showed their white teeth in grins. Then they said good-bye and started. The Honorable Davy carried along a big bundle of red, white and blue patriotism and a few hurricane speeches tied up in an alligator hide. He rode on Old Mississippi, with Death Hug waddling along behind. This caused a good deal of talk along the way, and at times people wondered who this fellow was. Sometimes, it was claimed, he told them:

"I'm the yallerest blossom in the forest. I can wade the brown Mississippi, jump the Ohio, step across the Obion River, ride a streak of lightning, slip without a scratch down a thorn tree, whip my weight in wildcats, put a rifle ball through the moon, and eat any man opposed to Jackson."

This, as you might expect, rather impressed people.

At one place, Davy had killed a bear and was cooking himself a bear steak when he heard a noise in the bushes where he'd put down his bundle. A panther had picked it up and was running away with it. He took off like a bolt of lightning, caught the critter, wrestled with him, and got the bundle back.

This was lucky, since without it he couldn't have brought the big wind he did to Washington.

That's the story people told about the way he went to Congress.

Whether Davy got to Washington this way or not (and some historians say he went there by stage-coach, not on Old Mississippi) he got there.

Washington wasn't much of a place yet. The streets hadn't been paved, and the mud or the dust, depending on the weather, was hub deep or a little deeper, except in spots where the streets were over-grown with grass. Cows pastured on many of them. The buildings and houses were scattered, and even on the best streets they had wide spaces between them, like Grampa Crockett's teeth.

Davy found it a strange place, and in turn, Washington found him a strange man. He was soon famous as "the coonskin congressman"—the first of his kind on the scene. Stories about him were told everywhere and were printed in the newspapers by those that liked him and those that didn't.

He soon saw one plain fact about Washington, and told about it.

"There's too much talk," he said. "Many men seem to be proud they can say so much about noth-ing. Their tongues keep working, whether they've any grist to grind or not. Then there are some in

110

Congress who do nothing to earn their pay but listen day after day. But considering the speeches, I think they earn every penny, amounting to eight whole dollars a day—provided they don't go to sleep. It's harder than splitting gum logs in August, though, to stay awake."

(When you come on a remark like that about the United States Congress, you can be thankful things have changed and aren't like that any more, so congressmen tell me, anyhow.)

Congressman Crockett himself didn't talk much in Congress, though he did manage as a rule to stay awake and decide which way to vote, and vote that way. But there were two big arguments he got into, and he spoke out what he felt about them.

One was about public lands. This trouble had a beginning a long way back in the past. Even before the Revolution, some men had come into the western country, including Tennessee, and got hold of tracts of land there, hoping to sell them at a profit when settlers moved in. Then after the Revolution, veterans had been given rights (in the form of warrants) to good tracts, provided they settled them. The speculators had bought warrants from the veterans, and they claimed a good many tracts that no veteran had ever seen. Well, after that, many settlers had come in, had got what they thought were sound claims to parcels of land, had cleared them and started to farm them. The next thing they knew, speculators swarmed in and claimed the land. Another thing, the state government began to want title to the lands which hadn't been taken, so it could sell tracts and raise money. And to do this, a survey was started, to find what lands could be taken over.

Congressman Crockett, who'd cleared land many times and knew what a chore it was, fought against the high taxes levied to pay for the survey and fought for the policy of selling the land for low prices, at easy terms, to the settlers who'd cleared it.

"The settlers," he said, "have been robbed by the speculators. They've had to move to land so poor, often, it wouldn't even raise a fight. Now they're being taxed to pay for this survey, and many can't pay the tax. I've seen the last blanket of an honest, hard-working family auctioned off under the hammer to pay for that survey. Next, these men who have broken the cane and cleared the land, they're going to be driven from their land by the high prices put on it, so more speculators can make a profit. Everything they've got is to be grabbed from them for the purposes of speculation. A swindling machine is to be set up to strip them of what little the surveyors and the warrant holders have left them.

112

It'll never be said that I sat by in silence and watched this thing done."

Crockett had been elected as a backer of Andrew Jackson, who was now President. Jackson was on the other side in this argument. So this was the beginning of a break between Congressman Crockett and the man who'd led him at the time of the Creek War. Davy was licked in the fight; but just the same, he got things handled so the settlers benefited by his standing up for them. The action was put off for eleven years, and when it was taken, the settlers got rights they couldn't have got if Davy hadn't led the fight.

The other big battle the Tennessee congressman got into was also about land rights—Indian land rights. Again, the history of the fight went far into the past. As far back as 1785, treaties had been made with the Cherokee Indians which said they were a nation, and that they owned certain lands, and that they could make the laws there. These were the first of a series of treaties, not only with the Cherokees but also with the Choctaws, Chickasaws, Seminoles and Creeks along the same line, giving the tribes the rights to their lands forever. General Jackson himself had signed a treaty giving such rights.

Beaten though they'd been in 1813 and 1814, the Indians had been doing very well on the lands they'd

113

been left after the war. The Creeks and Cherokees in Georgia, the Choctaws and Chickasaws in Mississippi and Alabama, and the Cherokees in Tennessee had kept their word about not going on the warpath again. The Cherokees had farmed, they'd raised cattle, they'd even woven cloth and built some roads—and the other tribes had done almost as well.

But the settlers wanted some of the good land for farming, and gold was discovered on some Indian land. Another thing, the whites had an old habit of breaking treaties with the Indians. So the states began to do what they could to get the Indians to move, and Jackson backed a bill to help them. The bill said the Indians could "exchange" their lands for lands west of the Mississippi, and it set up a fund of five hundred thousand dollars to help the Indians move.

You'd probably expect Davy to favor such a bill. His grandfather and grandmother had been killed by Indians; he'd seen the Red Sticks shoot down his friends; and he himself had had hard times fighting them. But Davy forgot any old grudges and stood up for what were clearly the rights of his Indian neighbors.

"I'm a man," he said, "with very humble abilities—haven't been to school more than six months altogether. You might figure I'd keep my

mouth shut and vote. Moreover, I know many congressmen from my state and from states near to it are
for the bill, and I'd like to go along with them. But
I've got to do what my conscience says is just and
right, whatever comes of it.

"Now I've always viewed the native Indian tribes
of this country as a sovereign people. They've been
said to be from the time our government started. The
United States is bound by treaty to protect them. I
can't go for a law that breaks a rule going back to the
time our nation signed its first treaties with the Indians. The only chance these poor people—once so
powerful—the only chance they have is to get help
in Congress. If we turn a deaf ear to them, misery
will be their fate.

"No man can be more willing than I am to see
these people move, if they can do it in a manner
that's agreeable to them. But I won't be willing
otherwise. I know the Chickasaw tribe: they're right
on the border of my district. They don't want to
move. I know part of the Cherokees don't want to
go. I heard them with my own ears say, 'No. We'll
take death here at our homes. Let them come and tomahawk us here. We're willing to die, but not to
move.' I can't go for a bill that will drive off the Indians against their will.

"If I'm the only member of the House to vote

against this bill—yes, if I'm the only man in the whole country against it, I'll still vote against it. It'll be a matter of rejoicing to me till the day I die that I've voted as I intend."

It wasn't, by the standards of those times, a great speech. Those were the days when Daniel Webster, with his thundery voice and his flowery style, and Edward Everett, with his even fancier one, were thought to be the best at speech-making. But it came from the heart, and in any time, that's more important than a fine style or, in fact, anything else. (A full report of Davy's speech, if you'd like to read it, may be found on page 181).

So there was a good deal of talk about the speech in the newspapers. And societies such as the Quakers, and a number of great men backed up the congressman's stand. But nearly everybody was for Jackson at that time; he was for the bill, and it was passed. In time, the Indians had to move: they called the trail they took "the Trail of Tears." Many of them suffered hardships; some even died. So Davy's guess worked out, and something happened that Americans aren't too happy to remember.

The next election, Jackson and the people in his party were still against Davy, so he was beaten. This was in 1831. To show how such things go, though, he ran again in 1833, and won.

The second time he went to Washington, he was even more famous than the first. This was partly because he'd made such a stir the first time, partly because by now there were so many stories going around about him, partly because Americans (or almost any other people, come to think of it) have always liked to laugh, and except when there was serious business to deal with, he did what he could to help them laugh.

Just the way Davy's neighbors had once told any number of stories about him, the newspapers kept printing yarns they'd picked up one place or another.

For example, there was the one about his trip to a circus in Washington. Soon after he got in, it went, he had a look at some wildcats. As it happened, one turned over and died, right away. The keeper came running. "Stranger, you're wasting your time," Davy told him. "My looks kill those things. You'd better pay me to get out of here, or I'm likely to kill every varmint you've got."

Next thing, a lion began to roar. "Turn him out," says Davy. "I'll whip him for a ten-dollar bill."

Davy wandered over to another part of the show, where a monkey was riding a pony.

Someone said, "Crockett, doesn't that monkey favor President Jackson?"

"No," Davy answered him back, "but he is the

spittin image of Major Wright of Ohio."

Just then, the congressman turned around and saw Major Wright, about three feet away. Davy found this a little awkward, but he bowed to the company and said, "I've either slandered the monkey or the major, and if you'll tell me which, I'll beg the other's pardon."

Everybody laughed. But the next day a fellow came up and told Davy that Major Wright was going to challenge him to a duel. Davy thought duels silly (as they were), so he said, "Well, if I'm challenged, I take it I'll have the choice of weapons, so you can tell him I'll choose bows and arrows."

There were stories too about Congressman Crockett dining at the White House. One went that when the butler shouted "Make way for Colonel Crockett!" he answered him back, "Don't bother. Colonel Crockett can make way for himself." Another had it that when he was served some ice cream, which was a new thing in those days, at a White House dinner, he tasted it and whispered to his neighbor, "The cream is very tasty; but General Jackson will be most mortified when he finds out it's frozen." Still another story claimed he liked his first ice cream so well he ordered some of it to be sent by stagecoach back home to the Crockett children.

Some of the stories were in his favor, and some

were against him, depending on how the newspapers stood. So, many people became eager to find out exactly what sort of a man he was. His party (the one against Jackson) decided that he'd attract big crowds if he made a tour, and that his speeches might help in the coming election. So in the spring of 1834, he made a long tour—to Baltimore, Philadelphia, New York, Providence, Boston, and other places. The crowds were huge everywhere, and now and then a newspaper would say that people were surprised when, instead of a character out of a joke book, a fine-looking man came before them. One paper, for instance, said:

Many guesses were made about his personal appearance. Some supposed that he would not appear to be a man, but would have the form of some comical or ugly monster. Needless to say, such were disappointed. He seemed to us to look very much like other great men— shrewd, intelligent, graceful, with a dignified, manly face. He was not dressed in frontier buckskins. He wore dark plain clothes, and his large white shirt collar turned over a small neckerchief. He wore a broad-brimmed white hat. He has rosy cheeks, tanned by the out-of-doors, and his eyes sparkle with humor and fun.

Davy was as busy as ever in Congress, taking his

stand on the measures coming up. An interesting thing was that he wrote many letters and (with some help from a fellow congressman) wrote and published his autobiography, *A Narrative of the Life of David Crockett of Tennessee*. Anyone who studies what he wrote over the years, in letters for instance, will see that this unschooled man made great progress: he taught himself to say things better and in better handwriting all the time.

When the session was ended, he went home, stopping now and then in Pennsylvania, Ohio and Kentucky to make speeches, again to great crowds.

Back in Tennessee, he started a campaign for re-election. A widespread story had it that he told the voters in his district, "If you see fit to re-elect me, I will serve you as faithfully as I have done; but if not, you may go to hell, and I will go to Texas."

Whether he said this or not, (and he once told an audience that he did), it is a fact that before very long, ex-Congressman Crockett was heading for Texas and the Alamo.

7

"REMEMBER THE ALAMO!"

DOWN TO THE YEAR when Davy lost that election, and for some time after, our country always had a frontier or two out West where a man could make a new start. For a good while, it had been Kentucky, Tennesse, Mississippi—along in there. In the year he was defeated, it was Illinois, Missouri and Arkansas and points west, mainly Texas. In New England, the old deep South, and (even more often) in Tennessee and Kentucky, a fair sprinkling of men were pinning notes or scrawling letters on the doors of their old shops or houses, and lighting out. The letters that they wrote were G.T.T., and everybody knew what they meant—GONE TO TEXAS.

A couple of Presidents had offered to buy Texas. Mexico (to which Texas belonged) turned its nose up and turned the Presidents down. Just the same, Mexico wanted settlers from the United States.

121

Some years back, Emperor Augustin I had told Stephen F. Austin to come along and bring in a couple hundred American families, and they could have a great tract of fertile land. A bit later, the Mexican Congress had said they'd give sixty-six thousand acres of land free to any other American that could get two hundred more American families to come and settle. No one collected on this, but by the time Davy lost that election, there were about eighteen thousand migrants from the United States, plus two thousand slaves, in Texas. The terms were very attractive. A family of pioneers could buy, say, four thousand acres for a few pennies an acre, then have nothing to do but clear them, cultivate them, and help the Mexicans fight any hostile Indians that dropped by.

You know how Americans—especially in Texas—always gripe about their *own* government. You can imagine, then, how cantankerous the settlers were about a *Mexican* government. They didn't like the way it got itself overthrown so often, didn't like its tariff system, didn't like its immigration laws. The Americans were coming more and more to think that the only thing to do was to start a revolution, take over Texas and run her right.

The last day of October, 1835, Davy wrote one of his brothers: "I am on the eve of starting to the

Texes. [He meant "the Texas"; but Davy never was one to let spelling teachers decide how *he'd* write a word.] Myself, Abner Burgin, and Lindsy K. Tinkle, and our nephew William Patton from the lower country—this will make our company. We will go through Arkinsaw and I want to explore the Texes well before I return."

This letter shows that, contrary to what some people think, Davy didn't go to Texas to get into a war: he went to look things over, very probably with the idea of making another move westward if he liked what he saw.

There's a story that Davy was so stirred up by the thought of leaving Tennessee, he went and wrote a poem for the first time in all his born days. This is the way they say it went:

Farewell to the mountains whose mazes to me
Were more beautiful far than Eden could be;
No fruit was forbidden, but Nature had spread
Her bountiful board, and her children were fed.
The hills were our garners—our herds wildly grew,
And Nature was shepherd and husbandman too.
I felt like a monarch, yet thought like a man,
And I thanked the Great Giver, and worshiped his
  plan.

123

The home I forsake where my offspring arose:
The graves I forsake where by children repose.
The home I redeemed from the savage and wild;
The home I have loved as a father his child;
The corn that I planted, the fields that I cleared,
The flocks that I raised, and the cabin I reared;
The wife of my bosom—farewell to ye all!
In the land of the stranger I rise—or I fall.

Farewell to my country!—I fought for thee well,
When the savage rushed forth like the demons from
  hell.
In peace or in war I have stood by thy side—
My country, for thee I have lived—would have died!
But I am cast off—my career now is run,
And I wander abroad like the prodigal son—
Where the wild savage roves, and the broad prairies
  spread,
The fallen—despised—will again go ahead!

Well, it's a very touching poem, and it'd be pleasant to think Davy composed it without any practice. Anyone who wants to believe this can go ahead and do so. It's a free country.

No one can be sure whether the men Davy spoke of in his letter went with him, though it is sure that if they did, they didn't stick with him all the trip. With these men or alone, he went down the Obion River and boarded a steamer at Mills Point. The boat was long and trim and fine for travel. The two chimneys had tops cut to look like crowns of plumes, and were painted fire-wagon red. Some kind of a gadget painted gold swung between them, and black smoke just billowed out and trailed behind them. The pilot house was all glass and curlicues. The paddle box had the sun painted on it. All the decks had spic-and-span white railings with filagree decorations. Men with ruffled shirts, tail coats and high hats, and ladies with parasols and billowy flowered dresses walked the decks and peeked over the railings. The boat went down the Mississippi, then up the Arkansas River to Little Rock, Arkansas Territory.

Little Rock, everybody told Davy, was growing like fury: only four years back, she'd been made a town, and soon she was to be chartered as a city. In Little Rock, Davy made one of his speeches, beat the best marksman in those parts in a shooting match, and went to a banquet. Then he went to Fulton.

There he stopped long enough to have a look at the nearby countryside, to hunt with some of the settlers, and since he was low on funds, to sell his gold watch. He and some friends—possibly those named in his letter—left Fulton on a dinky teakettle of a steamer and went up the curvy Red River to Natchitoches. Since it was early January by now, the river was high, and the dumpy little boat had to puff and chug like fury to shove its way through waters red with silt.

The party bought horses in Natchitoches and set out for Nacogdoches. These two towns, by the way, were said to have been started up by two Indian brothers. *Natchitoches* meant *pawpaw eaters* and *Nacogdoches* meant *persimmon eaters*. This showed that the brothers had different tastes, I suppose, but many settlers must have felt they weren't different enough. The Indians, of course, didn't care how much trouble people would have spelling or pronouncing these names or telling the danged places apart.

Davy and his friends trotted along what had been Camino Real (the King's Highway), now called the Spanish Trail. It meandered over rolling hills and through thick forests. In places, I'll say (if you'll excuse me), this was more of a trial than a trail, for it tended to get lost. If they hunted long enough, though, they'd find blazed trees and take their bearings from them.

The first thing they saw in Nacogdoches, so the story goes, was a flag flying on a high liberty pole. Drums were beating and fifes were playing, and people were marching or larruping around.

"Is this in our honor?" Davy asked one of them.

"Well, not exactly. A couple of officers of the Texan government were took prisoners by the Mexicans. They got away, and they're back, and that's what we're celebrating. But now you're here, we'll make it a double celebration."

So they fired a cannon in Colonel Crockett's honor, and invited him to the banquet.

This was early in January, 1836. While Davy'd been traveling, they told him, the Texans had got their revolution rolling. They'd heaved the Mexican garrison out of San Antonio de Bexar (Bexar for short); they'd organized a government; and they'd asked Americans to come help them. Now they had composed an "Oath of Allegiance" for people to sign, saying they'd be true to the government or any later government, and help it all they could. Davy read it over.

"Sure, I'll sign this," he told them, "if you'll put in one word. Where it says, 'I will bear allegiance to any future government that will be declared,' just you make it read 'future *republican* government,' will you? That's the only kind I go for."

A few days later, he was in nearby San Augustine, writing his son and daughter a letter:

My dear Son and Daughter:

This is the first time I have had the opportunity to write to you with convenience. I am now blessed with excellent health, and am in high spirits, although I have had many difficulties to encounter. I have got through safe and have been received by everybody with open arms of friendship, I am hailed with a hearty welcome to this country, a dinner and a party of Ladys have honored me with an invitation to participate with them, both in Nacogdoches and this place: the cannon was fired here on my arrival and I must say as to What I have seen of Texas, it is the garden spot of the world, the best land & best prospects for health I ever saw is here; there is a world of country to settle, it is not required to pay down for your league of land; every man is entitled to his headright of 4438 Acres and they may make the money to pay for it off the land.

I expect in all probability to settle on the Bodark or Chocktaw Bayou of Red River, that I have no doubt is the richest country in the world, good land, plenty of timber, and the best springs, and good mill streams, good range, clear water & every appearance of health—game a plenty. It is the pass where the buffalo passes from the north to south and back twice a year and bees and honey a plenty.

I have a great hope of getting the agency to settle

that country and I would be glad to see every friend I have settle there, it would be a fortune for them all. I have taken the oath of the government and have enrolled my name as a volunteer for six months, and will set out for the Rio Grande in a few days with the volunteers of the U.S., but all volunteers are entitled to a vote for a member of the convention and these members are to be voted for; and I have little doubt of being elected a member to form the Constitution for the Provence. I am rejoiced at my fate. I had rather be in my present situation than to be elected to a seat in Congress for life. I am in great hopes of making a fortune for myself and family bad as has been my prospects . . . . I hope you will do the best you can and I will do the same. Do not be uneasy about me I am with my friends. I must close with great respects.

Your affectionate father, Farewell
David Crockett

So Davy thought as well of Texas as all Texans (to put it mildly) do—even brand-new ones. At this stage, he liked her because she had the best of everything he went for.

When Davy told an old-timer what he'd written, though, they say the man told him: "When you've been here longer, like us, you'll be fond of her not only because she has the best but also because she has the worst. She's so big, you know, that she has room for all kinds of soil and several climates. Anybody that stays here long gets broiled by the sun in the summer and friz by the northers in the winter; has a look at the purtiest and the ugliest people and places, and takes turns starving and feeding high on the hog.

"Even in the same place," the old-timer went on, "things go from the worst to the best, or the other way around, mighty fast. There's a story about a fellow down here that shot two deer, both bucks as I recall. He went hunting on a cold winter day after a real dry summer. He saw a buck propping his self against a tree and shot it. It looked the same, but when he got close, he saw he'd killed it. The ball had gone through a hide as dry and brittle as a wooden slat, and no blood came from the wound. There wasn't any meat at all. When he picked the critter up, the horns fell off, a breeze came up quick and blew it out of his hands, and bones fell rattling on the ground. Only use he could make of it was to bust it into bits and use it as flints for his gun.

"On the same spot, two months later, on a fine spring morning, he killed another buck. The ball heated up the fat so steam pored from the hole it made, and the ball was melted. The critter bled so,

130

the man had to dig a trench to drain the blood away. He needed the help of four men to load the carcass on a wagon and of four mules to carry it home. When his knife cut the hide, it popped and slipped off like the skin off a Concord grape. He fed the whole family on the meat for a week and boiled the fat into ten barrels of soap. That's Texas for you: when she ain't the worst, she's the best."

Davy got a chance to see some proof of this in the next four weeks while he rambled around southeastern Texas recruiting men and getting together provisions for the Tennessee Mounted Volunteers. There are stories about four men that a writer said—joined him:

The first man he met aboard the little Red River steamboat on the way to Natchitoches. Seeing a crowd at one end of the boat, Davy joined them. They were watching a lanky fellow in a black suit, a ruffled shirt and a tall white hat. He sat on a chest shuffling three thimbles about, rolling a pea from thimble to thimble.

"Come on," he said. "Take a chance at thimblerig. All you do to win my money is name the thimble the pea's under." Seemed the trick was harder than it looked, because he was picking up shillings as fast as a hen pecks chicken feed. "Here, stranger," he told Davy, "you take a chance."

"I'm principled against betting money, but," he said, "I don't mind going in for drinks for the present company."

"Very well," Thimblerig said, and he chattered on while shifting the pea and the thimbles.

Davy's eye was keen as a lizard's, and he'd seen what the man was doing: if anyone guessed the right thimble when he lifted it, he'd make the pea disappear by sleight of hand. This time, when he stopped, Davy said, "It's under the middle thimble." But when the man reached to lift the thimble, Davy said, "Stop, if you please! I'll lift it." The pea was there, and Thimblerig had to treat.

Later Davy talked to the fellow. He was a rascal, he admitted straight off. He'd been raised a gentleman, but when he'd lost his fortune he'd gone on the stage, where he'd done badly. Then he'd been a gambler in New Orleans and Natchez. Now he was downhearted and discouraged, and didn't know what to do.

"Well," says Davy, "why don't you come on to Texas and make a new start there? There's room enough and to spare, even for the worst of us." So the man agreed, and became one of the colonel's party.

The second man Davy met late one evening when he was strolling down the street in Natchitoches. At

132

the time he first saw him, the fellow was leaning against a signpost, singing a sweet song to the empty street. He was a handsome young man with skin as brown as mahogany. He wore a tilted fur hat, fringed buckskin hunting clothes and polished boots. Another man—a huge fellow—came up and started to yell insults at him. The young fellow hardly paused in his singing. He handed Davy his rifle, then his hunting knife, then picked up the big fellow—for all his size—as calm as ever you please, carried him over to a watering trough, dumped him in, and pumped water over him.

After his victim had squished away, looking more sheepish than a sheep does, the young man came back and said, "Colonel Crockett, I know you from your pictures. I'll thank you for my rifle and my knife now. I've been looking for you. I'm Ned Johnson, a bee hunter by trade, at your service. If you're agreeable, I'd like to sign as a volunteer and go to Texas with you."

According to the story, the third and fourth men Davy met after he, Thimblerig and Ned Johnson had crossed the Trinidad River and had stopped at a hut for the night. This pair got there soon after, also wanting to stay the night. One was a tall, heavily bearded fellow dressed in a sailor suit, and with a tarpaulin on his head. His hair was black and long.

He had a scar on his forehead and another on the back of one hand. The other was a young Indian in a buckskin hunting suit. The bee hunter, who'd met them, told Davy that the sailor had been a pirate under the famous Lafitte, and the Indian was an escaped slave from down Galveston way. They looked about as tough and able to care for themselves as any men Davy'd ever seen, so he was willing and glad to have them join the volunteers.

These—or people like them—along with some doctors, lawyers, and civil engineers (so some historians say) made up the group that in early February rode away with Davy. News had spread that a Mexican army with Mexico's top general, a fellow named Antonio Lopez Santa Anna in command, was marching to Bexar, to try to get back and reopen this doorway into Texas. Bexar had been the chief Mexican stronghold in Texas for all of a hundred years. Most Texans figured that if the enemy retook it, they could go rolling on to the Sabine River without let or hindrance. So, with a troop of volunteers (the best guess is twelve of them), Davy headed for Bexar and the Alamo.

February 7 or 8, they got to Bexar—a little town standing in the bright sun out there in the middle of nowhere. Except for a few American families, most of the townspeople were Mexicans. About a half mile northeast of the town the party came to the Alamo, a low gray building with the Texas flag (red, white and green, with the numerals 1824 on its white bar) flying at its southwest corner. There were very few traces that showed that the Alamo had been a deserted mission before it had been turned into a fort. Ditches had been dug or deepened around it, walls had been banked with dirt to ward off cannon balls. Roofs had been torn off and scaffolding set up so cannons and soldiers could stick their noses over the tops of the walls, as some were doing at the moment the party got there.

When the Volunteers went galloping through the big door of the fortress, the men inside raised a cheer. They'd have cheered anybody, because soon after the Alamo'd been taken from the Mexicans, only a small force had been left there—and they were now hoping for reinforcements.

A tall young man with crisp red hair and a beard to match, dressed in an officer's uniform, came up and shook Davy's hand.

"We heard you're expecting some trouble," Davy told him. "My name's Crockett—David Crockett."

"Lieutenant-Colonel William Barret Travis, at your service. Your fame spread ahead of you: we heard you were coming with these volunteers. We expect trouble, and soon now. For some time, we had rumors that General Santa Anna was marching on us with no one knew how many men. Four days ago I learned from a friend whom I trust that the general is camped on the Rio Grande with two thousnad men, and that five thousand are a little back and marching on. We've sent out requests again and again for more men and supplies, but we don't get them." Travis had a soft Southern accent, and the mannerly way he talked showed why newspapers kept calling him "the gallant Travis."

By this time, news that Davy Crockett was on hand had spread all over the little fort, the way news spreads among soldiers, you know, and always has. Soldiers poured out of the barracks and started yelling "Speech! Speech!" So Davy gave them a short talk which it is said went this way:

"Gentlemen: We're glad to be here and we thank you for your welcome. I've come here to prove I'm a true Texan, though for a fact, it looks like I've picked a mighty bad time to do this. I've been duly elected Congressman from my district in Tennessee, as you may know. I don't mention this because I want votes; I don't intend to run, either for office or for safety. I mention it because I want to tell you I'm after an even higher honor now. That's the honor of being a private in this garrison and defending the liberty of the country. I and my men are from Tennessee and Kentucky, and we aim to prove that those states deserve the name they have for rearing up men that are half horse, half alligator, and can give a good account of themselves in a fight."

Soon Colonel James Bowie, co-commander of the fortress, came up and introduced himself. He'd come, like Davy, from Tennessee. This pale, chestnut-haired man looked too thin to be much of a fighter; but the talk was that with his bowie knife he'd killed a man fighting him with a sword, and that as a Texas Ranger he'd earned the nickname, "The Fighting Devil." For all this, he was as quiet-spoken a man as you'd ever meet.

A little talk made it clear that the garrison was in a most uncomfortable fix. In the Texas government there were all sorts of disagreements and feuds; and no one with real power had done anything to be very helpful to the force of only about a hundred and fifty able men at the Alamo. General Sam Houston, as a matter of fact, had wanted Bexar evacuated and the fortress blown up. But Bowie had decided the order was wrong. "We'd rather die in these ditches," he wrote, "than give up to the enemy." Travis, though he didn't agree with Bowie about some other matters, was of the same mind.

In the days after the volunteers' arrival, the officers kept sending out scouts to spy on Santa Anna, and messengers to learn if the defenders of the fort couldn't get help. The officers and the men did some more work to get ready for the enemy. They herded some beeves into an enclosure, and brought in supplies. They mounted more guns, bringing up the number to eighteen. Where there was a break in a wall, they put an eight-pounder. They saw to it that the two aqueducts that brought in water were in good shape.

The news was that on the night of February 20, Santa Anna camped on the Medina River. A cold norther blew up a storm that kept him from crossing that night or the next. But the night of February 22, a good share of the Mexicans living in the town went away. The Americans all were ordered into the fort. Two scouts saw the Mexican cavalry camped on the hills to the west looking down on the city, and galloped to the fort. Riding into the enclosure, the scouts met Crockett, who went with them to Travis to report.

"I must send a message to Gonzales as soon as possible so as to rally the people to my support," Travis said. He got the two scouts started.

Davy, still standing by, said, "And here I am, Colonel. Assign me to some place, and I and my Tennessee boys will defend it all right."

"Good. You and your men are to defend the picket wall up there on the south side, running to the corner of the church."

By three o'clock in the afternoon of February 23, the Mexicans had taken Bexar and had raised a red flag on the San Fernando church. (The red flag was the Mexican way of saying, "We'll give no quarter.") The garrison gave a cannon shot as its answer, and the seige was on.

A letter Travis smuggled out of the fort the next day told how things went the first twenty-four hours and again asked for help:

Commandancy of the Alamo.
Bejar, Feb'y 24th, 1836.

To the People of Texas and all Americans in the World.

Fellow Citizens and Compatriots: I am besieged, by a thousand or more of the Mexicans under Santa Anna. I have sustained a continual bombardment and cannonade for 24 hours and have not lost a man. The enemy has demanded a surrender at discretion, otherwise, the garrison are to be put to the sword, if the fort is taken. I have answered the demand with a cannon shot, and our flag still waves

139

proudly from the walls. I shall never surrender or retreat. Then, I call on you in the name of Liberty, of patriotism and everything dear to the American character, to come to our aid with all dispatch. The enemy is receiving reinforcements daily and will no doubt increase to three or four thousand in four or five days. If this call is neglected I am determined to sustain myself as long as possible and die like a soldier who never forgets what is due to his own honor and that of his country. VICTORY OR DEATH.

WILLIAM BARRETT TRAVIS,
Lt. Col. Comdt.

The siege went on for days and days which seemed like centuries and centuries. The Mexicans kept up a cannonade—kept it up, so Travis reported, "incessantly." Early in the siege, Bowie was forced to go to bed with typhoid-pneumonia, and Travis was left in command. Now and then, at night, the Americans would dash out, get some wood or supplies, then hurry back into the fort. Now and then a detachment of Mexican soldiers would rush toward the fort and be driven back.

Crockett, so Travis reported, "was seen at all points, animating the men to do their duty." A story is that, in lulls in the fighting, the colonel entertained

140

the men by playing a fiddle, by telling some of his famous stories, and by singing a song to the Mexicans—"Won't You Come Into My Bower?"

The days and nights stretched endlessly. On March 1, hope flickered up for a while when thirty-two men sent as reinforcements from Gonzales came through the enemy lines and into the fort. Hope was quenched, though, when Travis learned that this was all the help he'd be getting from Gonzales, and that he'd be getting no help at all from any other point in Texas. This meant that a force of about a hundred and eighty men faced the job of defending the fort when at least a thousand were needed to succeed. And ammunition was getting low, and there was no sign the garrison would get more.

On March 3, legend says, Travis got the men together. He said: "I've called you here to tell you plain truth and to let you make a choice. We have been begging and hoping for reinforcements. I know now that no more aid is coming. When the final assault comes—and it may come any hour now—it will mean death to all of us in the fort. I will stay until the end and die fighting. Now, I draw a line— [He scratched a long line on the ground.] Those of you who want to leave will not be hindered. You still have a chance to save yourselves. Those of you who will stay, step across to my side of the line."

The story is that there was silence for a minute, then the men began to shuffle across the line. Even Colonel Bowie, sick though he was, insisted that they carry him across on his bed. Some say that in all the garrison, only one man didn't cross the mark, others say that every man crossed it.

All the time, the Mexican army had been growing. All the time, they'd come closer and closer to the walls of the Alamo. By March 5, General Santa Anna had forces of five thousand, outnumbering the Texans by forty-eight hundred or so. Now there were hardly any gaps in the ring of Mexicans and cannons. There were fewer letups in the shooting, too.

Santa Anna readied a final attack. By his orders, the battalions were divided into four columns. Each column had its scaling ladders, its axes, its crowbars. The cavalry was to be in the rear, to back up the infantry wherever it was needed.

At ten o'clock, the night of March 5, of a sudden every Mexican gun was quiet. The Mexican forces moved back out of sight. After all the cannonading and rifle shots, there was a stillness that was unbelievable. The only sound was a little wind rustling the new green leaves on the nearby cottonwoods.

Men who've fought in long engagements say that after a few days and nights, a man sleeps a few minutes when the chance offers, but of course he never really can rest properly. Then if the action ends, or a tired man gets to a quiet place, nothing's likely to keep him from sleeping like a log. Well, the Texans had been at their posts practically all the time for eleven days and nights or more, and their eyelids were like lead. When this blessed spell of quiet came, though they tried hard, most of them couldn't keep their eyes open a minute longer.

"It's the lull before the storm, men," Travis—so the story goes—told them. "We'll have sentinels set. We'll post picket guards on the walls."

The Mexicans were quiet as a tomb up to the very start of the attack. Either the guards fell asleep or they were run upon and bayonetted, because they didn't sound an alarm.

Only one man seems to have been awake—a captain. His yell split the night. Outside, a bugle note sounded, then there was the rush and tramp of marching soldiers. Then Travis, with his rifle and his sword in his hands, was rushing for a cannon and yelling, "Come on, boys, the Mexicans are upon us!"

At this point, the Mexican band somewhere out there in the night started to play the *deguello*, a Spanish tune that from time out of mind had been a command to kill, plunder, burn and destroy without mercy. The Texans got to their posts, and the guns and cannons on the walls poured shots into the masses of men with scaling ladders milling below. Twice the men with the ladders were driven back. Then, just as the sun rose on a fine bright day—the last that many would ever see—the enemy managed to come over the walls. This was when Travis fell, a bullet in his forehead, beside a silenced cannon, his rifle in his hand. Legend has it that Crockett was in command for the rest of the fight.

Now the Mexicans swarmed over the walls and into the enclosures. Blasts of powder broke down some doors, battering rams broke down others, and the enemy were soon coming at the Texans from every side. The Americans shot their rifles or pistols as long as they could load them, then used them as clubs. There were a good many hand-to-hand struggles. But the Mexican forces were too overwhelming to fight off.

The story was that the whole American force of a hundred and eighty-three was killed. From ten to twenty women and children were all in the fort to survive. A good guess is that fifteen hundred and forty-four of a Mexican force of five thousand were killed or mortally wounded.

And legend says that Colonel David Crockett fell near the gate in the fifty-foot wall that joined the church to the long barracks. Many of the enemy were piled about him. Also, according to legend, the Tennessee Volunteers lay nearby in the section of the Alamo they'd been ordered to defend.

8

DID DAVY COME
THROUGH THE BATTLE?

AMERICANS in Texas and all over the United States took for granted that Davy had died with the others in the Alamo. Some survivors even said they'd seen his body with enemies he'd killed piled up about him. One counted eleven, another twenty-two.

The siege gave the Texans a battle cry—"Remember the Alamo!"

This was what the troops shouted on April 21, 1836, when General Sam Houston and his army tore into Santa Anna and his army in the battle of San Jacinto. They scattered the Mexican forces and took Santa Anna prisoner. This pretty well decided things at the time.

Ten years later, though, when there was another war with Mexico, Americans still remembered the Alamo and Crockett. One song they sang went:

The Siege of the Alamo—1848 Almanack

Remember gallant Crockett's bones
Have found a glorious bed there.
Then tell them in your thunder tones
No tyrants' feet shall tread there.

Back home, the neighbors believed Davy had died in the Alamo, and some went so far as to believe the animals thought so, too. One neighbor said:

"There's a great rejoicin' among the bears of Tennessee and Kaintuck, and the Mississippi River alligators have got so fat and lazy that they'll hardly move out of the way of a steamboat. The rattlesnakes frolic within ten feet of the clearin's. The foxes go to sleep in the goose-pens. It's all because the rifle of Crockett is stilled forever, and the print of his moccasin isn't found in our woods any more. His old coonskin cap hangs in the cabin, and nary a hunter looks at it without turnin' away his head and droppin' a tear.

"Luke Wing went into the cabin t'other day and took down one of Davy's old rifles. The muzzle was half stopped up with rust, and a great green spider ran out and made his escape. The varmints of the forest will fear it no more. The panthers and bears will miss him, but he never missed them.

"He died like a patriot ought to die. When he was about to do his country service and raise her name as high as the mountains, he was cut down in the prime of life. The whole country's clouded with darkness. If you want to see old Kaintuck's tears, go there and speak of the colonel. He's dead now, and may he rest forever and a day after."

Well, was he?

The question's worth raising, because if you think back, you'll recall that a good number of heroes didn't die when people thought they did. Offhand, I can think of King Arthur, Frederick Barbarossa, the French dauphin, Jesse James and Mark Twain. Well, Crockett was the equal of any of them, wasn't he?

Another thing: if people made a mistake thinking Davy was dead when he wasn't, it wasn't the first time. That time when Davy was twelve years old and ran away and didn't come back for three years, the whole family back at the tavern thought he was dead. But of course he wasn't.

Then there was the time in the fall of 1816 when he left his bride, Elizabeth, and the children behind while he went with some neighbors to look over the Creek country near where Tuscaloosa is now, thinking he might move there. The horses ran away in the night and he left his friends, to go after them. He waded creeks and swamps, climbed mountains, and went about fifty miles afoot in one day.

150

He got very sick and had to stop and lie abed in Jesse Jones' house for two whole weeks before he could go home.

"I was so pale, and so thinned down," says Davy—for he tells this himself, "that my face looked like it had been half soled with paper.

"When I got home, it was to the astonishment of my wife; for she thought I was dead. My neighbors who'd started with me had come back and took my horse home, which they'd found. They'd met men who said they'd seen me draw my last breath, and had helped bury me. Well, as soon as I heard it, I knew that was a whopping lie!"

Again, on February 22, 1836, *The Boston Evening Transcript* (a very respectable newspaper, even for Boston) had this story in it:

A letter has been received in Washington announcing the death of Col. Crockett, soon after his arrival in Texas.

Now back in those times before the telegram it took a fair number of days for news to get back East from Texas. So if Davy had died, it would have had to be early in February to get into a Boston paper February 22. You and I know, of course, that the siege of the Alamo started a day

151

after this, on February 23, and that Davy fought during the siege.

Here's another point: Soon after the siege—and long after it, too, for that matter—a story was all over Texas that five or more Texans came through the siege alive, and Davy was one of them. The story went on to say that they were lined up and shot.

For more than a century, this story was judged to be no more than a wild rumor. Then, when historians took a new hard look at the evidence, including some newly discovered and published, they decided that this ending to the story about the battle, and about Davy's fate, was the true one.

Clearly those who gave some accepted accounts of the massacre weren't the best possible authorities. Not one of the defenders of the Alamo had come out of the fort alive to tell what happened. True, the two informants who were depended upon and who were quoted at length had been in the Alamo during the siege. But since both had been in hiding throughout all the action, they hadn't had a chance to watch the fighting or the killings. The only surviving eyewitness had been Mexican soldiers. Although these had been rejected as unreliable, historians who reassessed the lot of them decided that some truly were the best sources of the truth about some of the happenings. One, for instance, had been a lieutenant in Santa Anna's army who had set down in his own private diary an unprejudiced account that now was translated into English and published. Another had been a sergeant who in the years after the Alamo battle had served in the Texas and the Confederate armies and who had been searchingly interviewed by some well qualified students of the battle. And important parts of the accounts given by this pair were verified by five Mexican soldiers who also had survived the siege.

Historians now generally agree that soon after the Alamo was seized, some Mexican soldiers came upon Davy Crockett and some other defenders of the fort, still alive and armed but exhausted and out of ammunition. The Mexicans tore the rifles out of the Americans' hands and took their captives to Santa Anna. The general gave a terse order: "Soldiers, kill them." One captive—some say it was Travis—grabbed a captor's gun and pushed it toward the floor. Other Mexicans opened fire. Arms folded, the prisoner and Davy stood straight and unflinching, staring defiantly at the Mexicans. They were shot down. So, as one of the group says, "The Americans died undaunted like heroes."

Although accounts that surfaced soon after these events contained some of the details that now are accepted as facts, hosts of stories that were told orally and printed later had Davy living a much longer time after the Alamo was seized than he actually did.

Here's a newspaper story from *The Boston Transcript*, May 3, 1836, copied down exactly:

COL. CROCKETT NOT DEAD

The Cincinnati Whig *states, on the authority of a gentleman who has arrived in Cincinnati from Texas, and who saw Col. Crockett three weeks previously, lying ill, at the house of his brother-in-law in Texas, that the Colonel was not dead, but that he was slowly recovering from his wounds.* The Whig *says:*

The gentleman who brings this news is known to a number of our citizens, who believe him to be a man of veracity. He states that Crockett was left upon the battleground at San Antonio, covered with wounds, and as the Mexicans supposed, dead. Then after the Mexicans had abandoned the place, Crockett was discovered by some of his acquaintances to be lying among the slain, still exhibiting signs of life. He was immediately taken care of, and conveyed to comfortable lodgings (as before stated), where his wounds were dressed, and every attention necessary to his recovery paid him. He had received a severe gash with a tomahawk on the upper part of the forehead, a ball in his left arm, and another through one of his thighs, besides several minor wounds. When the gentleman who brings this intelligence left his brother-in-law's house, Crockett was doing well.

Anyone who happens to have one of these old newspapers in an attic or a storeroom or some place can dig it out for himself and look over this evidence, in print, in a newspaper with a good reputation, that Colonel Crockett came through the horrible siege, and that he went on living after it.

And if he didn't get killed in 1836, so some reasoned, maybe he never did. Because you won't find a newspaper story anywhere that tells of his dying *after 1836*, right on down to the present time.

There's a final bit of evidence: For many years after 1836, neighbors in Tennessee, Kentucky, and in fact all over the country, told and published stories about Davy Crockett. Many of these told about things he did long after 1836. Even today, if you get far enough away from the highways and the cities and the hot-dog stands, you'll find people still spin yarns about Davy, and some of these yarns are about things that happened to him only a short time ago.

Now of course some of these stories are stretchers—maybe the lot of them are. Still they might have some truth in them: stories often do, you know.

9

DAVY AFTER THE ALAMO

T his chapter will now retell a few stories of the kind I mentioned a page ago—stories told after history said Davy was killed in the Alamo. They'll start early and come up to a fairly late date, and in that way they'll round out his biography properly.

Some stories go back to Davy's trip to Texas, and differ somewhat from the ones biographers tell. They hold that what made Davy eager to go to Texas was a report that a friend gave him about the land: "Why, Colonel Crockett, the soil's so rich if you plant a crowbar at night it'll sprout tenpenny nails before morning. It's deep, too. Some vegetables you just can't plant there, because the roots will go clear through the earth, and somebody in China will pull 'em out by the roots, and you'll waste all your work. I tell you, the land in Tennessee is just a frog pasture compared to the land in Texas."

This same friend told Davy something else that (it was said) made him want to go—that Texas had the best climate, handsomest women, bravest men, tastiest barbecues and loveliest señioritas in the world. (This, of course, was partly right.)

Again, it's claimed Davy didn't do all that traveling to get to Texas on steamboats and on horseback the way the biographers say he did. Instead, they tell that he rode on Death Hug's back, with Old Mississippi wallowing and snorting along behind. The only story that goes against this is the one told in Arkansas, where it's claimed he came to Little Rock riding on a catamount, with a bear under each arm, and that he left the same way. (I think, myself, that the people of Arkansas must have Davy mixed up with Pecos Bill: Davy as a rule didn't ride on a catamount, but Pecos Bill, another legendary Texan, did.)

Anyhow, one way or another, Davy got to Texas just in time to fight in the battle for the Alamo. Here he fought until his gun, old Betsy, was red hot. He then stopped bothering to take aim or pull the trigger, because, since it was so hot, it went off without help; and it was so well trained that it knocked over a Mexican soldier every time. He then was given four rifles to shoot, with two men to load them for him, and everyone brought down its man as fast as the two could load. After the ammunition was gone and the enemy had streamed over the walls, Davy fought with the breech of his musket until that was splintered, then with his knife until that was used up, and then with his fists. Result was, he licked the enemy as clean as a barked hemlock, and came through the siege fitter than a fiddle, and a first-rate fiddle at that.

Next, he began to race around Texas, hunting Mexican armies. He'd ride around on Old Mississippi or (more often) Death Hug and scare the armies away from where they were or—if they stood their ground—he'd at them with his hunting knife or with his rifle. It seems he traveled middling fast, since it's said that at one time the speed of Death Hug scalded all the hair from the poor bear's back and even set Davy's buckskins to smoking.

With his trusty rifle, old Betsy, Colonel Crockett helped supply rations the way he had in the Creek War. He shot enough buffaloes to feed the whole American army and some of their prisoners. "Never found anything I liked so well as this buffalo hunting. Bear hunting is child's play to it," Davy said. (Or so they tell us.)

He also found a way to cook buffalo steaks that pleased the best eating people in Texas. The wind would have to be blowing strong, and then there'd have to be a prairie fire whizzing along ahead of the whistling wind. Then Colonel Crockett would run along behind the fire and broil the steaks over the galloping flames. This gave the steaks a good smoky flavor and cooked them fast enough to save all the juice. They say Davy found that the steaks were cooked as well as any he'd eaten in any hotel in Washington when he was in Congress.

Texas, of course, had the biggest buffalo in the world down there. This beast kept up a noise like a thunderstorm, just by his breathing and bellowing, half the year round. Whenever the sky darked up in Texas, everybody knew the buffalo had scared away the sun. He was known as the Buffalo Devil, one that no critter would go for to come at. Davy went out specially to hunt him one day. He was a savagerous critter, Davy decided the minute he saw him, about twenty feet long and ten feet high. The story is that Davy came back to camp after the fight and said, "I could figure right off why they called him the Buffalo Devil. When he fixed his fire eye on me, he looked like a volcano acting up worse than usual. I first let my dogs fly at him, and that was a bad mistake. The critter gave one red-fire snort, and they were used up for life. This roused my ire, for I was very fond of those dogs. So I marched right up to him, pulled

160

out his tail by the roots, and beat him until he had to give up."

Though Colonel Crockett was most interested in buffaloes in Texas, he took care of many other animals down there. "There was a tract of a thousand acres," one Texan tells us, "where eight-foot rattlers were so thick no other earthly creature but birds could venture within a hundred yards of the spot without being cut up into rattlesnake chews. They used up more Indians than whisky. Davy walked in there and gave them fair warning: he clicked his teeth together by way of a rattle. They answered with a shake that would make you think all the trees were rattlesnakes. Then he waded into them, taking eight in each hand and cracking them of a sudden—whip fashion. Took their heads off, I'll swear. Heads everywhere, flying thick as snowflakes, till all the snakes were killed off. Saint Patrick couldn't have done it better."

Those are just samples of the critters the colonel killed or tamed or trained in Texas—not only buffaloes and snakes but also bears, wolves, panthers, wildcats, and a most unusual and fierce bird called the Texian Condor which in some ways was the worst of all.

Most of these adventures with animals in Texas must have come between 1835 and 1845, because

Davy on his Way to Texas
1845 Almanack

beginning in 1845, as you'd expect a veteran to be, the colonel was interested in the United States War with Mexico. Someone remembered a speech he made that went: "Hosses, [by which he meant Americans, I suppose], I am with you! While the stars and stripes wave in the breeze, where is the cowardly, low-lived, bristle-headed mother's son of you that won't smouse the citadel of the enemy and go ahead for liberty? Hosses, come along! Crockett's with you!" True to his word, he helped win this war, as he had two others. He seems to have got down to Mexico City, because we have a story about a battle he had with a lion in a bull ring down there.

Then, for a while, he was one of those fellows they call a "Good Will Traveler"—first one this country ever had.

"The first stop," a fellow tells us, "was Brazil. This was a country bigger than the United States, with a capitol on Sugar Loaf Mountain, and with more coffee, waterfalls and Brazil nuts than it could use up in a hundred years. But Brazil was having troubles with a river. One trouble was that the tigers and anacondas thought they owned the river. Another was that no one knew anything about it. Davy said he'd take care of both problems. The Brazilians figured this would be a big job, so they built a fleet of boats, canoes and all, for him to take the trip up the

163

Davy Explores the Amazon
1845 Almanack

river in. They painted the boats with Brazilian designs, all in bright colors.

"But when the Brazilians saw Crockett steer into their port on Old Mississippi, with Death Hug grunting and splashing behind, they saw that he was ready, without a fleet, to do the job himself. So they shot off a ninety-gun salute, he waved his measuring stick and his coonskin cap, Old Mississippi flipped his tail, and Death Hug waved his paw. They kept on going, a little faster than thinking, to find the end of the longest river in Brazil—Rio Medaria, I think they call it.

"It was a tough job. For one thing, it was a monstrous crooked river—so crooked that a steamboat on it (if there was one) could take on wood from one end of a woodpile in the morning, spend the day going around the curves, and then take more wood off the other end at night. For another thing, every now and then, all those vines and orchids and such hung down in a tight tangle close to the water, and the only thing for it was to swim under the water till you got past.

"Some places, where the current was fast, there wasn't one of them that could fight his way through without help. In a case like that, Davy and Death Hug would push Old Mississippi a few yards, and then Old Mississippi would go back and push Davy and Death Hug until they caught up with him.

"Coming back was easier, because Davy had measured most of the river on the way up, and because they could scoot along with the current. They would have to stop ever so often, though, and drive the anacondas and tigers away from the river. They also put up signs saying, PROPERTY OF BRAZIL—NO TIGERS OR ANACONDAS ALLOWED. (You may say animals can't read. Very well, why are there so many signs on American roads that say DEERS CROSS HERE, then?) They finished the whole job, measuring, drawing a picture of the river, and getting shut of the snakes and tigers, in sixteen days and thirteen seconds. The river was just twenty-three hundred miles and an ax handle long. The President or King or whatever it was of Brazil gave them all medals with ribbons on them."

Another stop on the Good Neighbor Tour was Haiti. The story doesn't say how Davy and his two pets got there; but we can assume that they either went by ship or swam, since this was before the time of airplanes.

Haiti looked like a crumpled piece of green paper that had been thrown into a tub of bluing water. The people there, when the heavy rain spoiled their roads, didn't fix the roads. "The Lord spoiled 'em," they'd say, "and the Lord will fix 'em up." They had bridges that were always falling down, so the first thing any visitor was always told was: "Never cross a bridge. Always go around it." Seven months of the year, the rain fell between half-past-one and fifteen minutes after five every afternoon. This was good for the sugar cane and coffee plants, as you can guess.

In Haiti, Davy, Death Hug and Old Mississippi met the Emperor, who had more feathers in his hat than seven Indians, and more shiny pins and stars on his coat than ten generals and the same number of play-actors (a total of twenty-seven people in all). Everybody in Haiti took off his hat and bowed down to him, and he was used to it.

So the first time Davy and his pets didn't do this, the Emperor looked puzzled.

"I," he said, "am Solok, the great and mighty Emperor of Haiti. How come you don't take off your hats and get down on your knees to me?"

Davy told him, "I'm just plain Davy Crockett, one of the humble rip-snorting nephews of Uncle Sam. And no nephew of Uncle Sam ever takes off his hat or kneels to any man this side of the sunshine. Neither does his pet bear or his pet alligator."

Solok found this interesting, and he invited Davy and the animals to come to the straw-topped palace

167

for a potluck dinner. Davy told him how it was, living in America. Then Solok gave a dance, with music made by some drums and calabashes. The music was so horrible that Davy had a hard time waiting for it to end so he could say he'd had a fine time and scoot away. (Good Will Ambassadors always have to say they've had a fine time.)

It says in the story that after Davy and the animals left the palace the great and mighty Solok sat there in the throne room, all alone except for forty-two dancers and ninety-four slaves. He sat there, with his chin in his hand, wishing that he could quit his job and be a humble rip-snorting nephew of Uncle Sam, like Davy, instead of a dad-blamed Emperor. But of course Solok hadn't had the right start in life or been brought up in the right place, and it was too late for him to begin all over again.

Davy seems to have got home again, some time or other. He lived in either Tennessee or Kentucky or Texas, more probably all three, the stories show. In Tennessee, he met up with some new neighbors who'd moved into the district while he was away—Skippoweth Branch, who slept in his hat and could scream through his nose, for instance, an interesting man to have around. Then there was a seagoing man named Ben Hardin, who had a dancing match with the Crockett girls that lasted all night and through the

Col. Crockett Beat in a Shooting Match   Almanack 1840

169

next day and wore out the stone steps in front of the Crockett cabin. He and Davy took some trips together, it seems, up to Oregon and to Niagara Falls and such places.

Either Davy lived in Kentucky or he was visiting there when he met Mike Fink, King of the Mississippi keelboatmen. The keelboatmen were the toughest men on the western rivers, and Mike was the champion of the lot. People said he could load a keelboat singlehanded, from stem to stern, in something less than thirty minutes, that he could turn a boat around on a drop of dew, and that he could pole, row, cordelle or bushwhack her upstream without any help. Mike said the same.

Seems he had a cabin on the Cumberland River, and Davy came to call on him. Mike made himself known in the usual way, telling what he was and what he could do: "I'm not only a horse and an alligator; I'm also crooked snags and red-hot snapping-turkle. I've got the handsomest wife, and the fastest horse, and the sharpest shooting iron in all Kentuck, and if any man dare doubt it, I'll be in his hair quicker than hell can scorch a feather!"

This got Davy's dander up, and says he, "I've nothing to say against your wife, and besides Mrs. Crockett's out of the state at the moment. I don't have a horse. But I'll just have a match with you to see whether you're mistaken aoout your shooting."

So they had a match. They drove nails into a tree, snuffed candles, and knocked flies off a cow's horn, and each man was as good as the other.

Then Mike looked over the field, and saw his wife, Sal, going after a gourdful of water. She had a high comb on her hair, and Mike blazed away. He knocked half the comb off, without stirring a hair. "Now," he said, "I'll give you a choice. Either you can shoot the half of that comb on again, or you can knock the other half off."

"No, no, Mike. David Crockett's hand would be sure to shake if his iron was pointed within a hundred yards of a female, and I give up beat."

They say this was the only time Davy was beaten in a shooting match and it was because he was so gallant and all.

All these things clearly happened some time ago. Now we come to more recent adventures it is said he had—well, sort of recent. He had this fight—or maybe two fights—with Halley's Comet. Here we've got some dates to deal with, because Halley's Comet came around in 1835, and then it didn't make a nuisance of itself again until 1910. Well, as I have said, there were stories about the way he fought the comet in 1835. But an important thing is, some of the facts about his tussle came out after the comet was around in 1910. So as good a guess as any had to be that he fought the thing two times—seventy-five years apart.

Halley's Comet, as the fellow that tells the story remembers it (and he was ten years old at the time it came along), just like lights on a Christmas tree, was red and blue and green. It took a jump and started lickety split for the earth. It scooted past stars and clouds, and kept right on coming.

Every night, as soon as the supper dishes were washed and the stock was watered, people would go out into the yard—front or back, whichever gave them the best view. They'd sit there in chairs or loll on blankets watching this bright blob up there dragging its tail behind it and getting bigger and bigger. The way it kept growing was disquieting.

In Washington, of course Senators, Congressmen, Cabinet Members, and the President began to get piles of letters about it. Both houses of course had committee meetings, took testimony, made speeches, and passed laws prohibiting the comet. But it paid them no heed—just kept sailing along, dragging its tail behind it, and getting bigger and bigger.

At last the President, after a long Cabinet meeting lasting into the night during which he posed for pictures looking concerned and (he hoped) reassuring, hit on an idea about what he could do. He put a story into the newspapers that said: *WANTED, by the President of the United States: Davy Crockett, to climb up to the top of a mountain and do something about Halley's Comet.*

Soon as he heard about this or happened to read about it in a newspaper, Davy followed his motto— made sure he was right and then went ahead. He went up to the top of Cloud Mountain. That was a high mountain: from its top on a clear day you could see to a point less than a mile from the eastern coast. Near the foot of Cloud Mountain was the Crockett cabin. Beyond that was Davy's pappy's cabin, standing there beside the Nolachucky River. The next river, the Mississippi, was so far off that it looked like a dirty string. Beyond this, there were several states and lakes and mountains and forests and cities that the geography books tell about.

At the proper time, the dark came. But Halley's Comet was shining so, and trailing so many sparks behind it, and coming so close, that it lit up the whole countryside and started a good many roosters crowing. The scenery with all that light shining onto it looked so handsome that it seemed sort of a shame to interfere with anything so ornamental as Halley's Comet was.

But Davy did what the President had asked him to do.

He waited until Halley's Comet came within reach, and then he grabbed it by the tail. It was a heavy comet; it had been swooping down a very long time; and the tail on the thing was an extra long one. So, as you can imagine, it was an obstreperous comet to handle. Davy had to plant his feet wide apart, curl his toes to keep a foothold, and move his tongue to the corner of his mouth. Then he swung it around his head seven times, to get up speed, you understand. About the sixth time it was pulling horribly hard, what with the centrifugal force (due, of course, to the inertia or something), but he scowled and swung it that one final time.

Then he let go.

The sparks flipped into the snow on top of Cloud Mountain, and hissed and steamed until they were smothered. And Halley's Comet scooted away in a new direction, past the clouds and past a large number of stars and planets. And the people sitting or lying out in their yards below were relieved to see that for a change it was getting smaller instead of bigger every minute.

(This rough treatment discombobulated a comet that—during several thousand years—had got set in its ways. So astronomers who spied on it through telescopes and figured how it'd orbit in 1985 and 1986 on its next visit could tell us not to worry. For this time it would miss the world by a good thirty-nine million miles. Seems Davy had taught it a lesson.)

Davy got his hands shockingly burned and had the hair singed off his head until he was as bald as an egg laid by a bald eagle. He had to roll in the snow in clouds of steam to put out the fire in the fringes of his hunting shirt. And afterwards, it's said, it took him a long time to grow himself a new crop of hair.

One windy story about Davy has been so much admired that I've decided to put it in here exactly the way it was first printed. This fine tall tale came out in one of the very popular *Crockett Almanacks* that were published annually in Nashville and later in many other scattered cities between 1834 and 1855. Along with calendars, weather predictions for the whole year, and other scientific stuff, these gave the world a great many pieces about Davy and other frontier characters. Though Davy had nothing to do with the earliest of these and less than nothing to do with the later ones, a good share of the tall tales were ascribed to him. The one that follows, though it probably was the creation of a New York free lance writer, purports to be in Davy's own words:

One January morning it was so all-screwen-up

175

cold that the forest trees war so stiff that they couldn't shake, and the very day-break froze as it war tryin' to dawn. The tinder-box in my cabin would no more ketch fire than a sunk raft at the bottom o' the sea. Seein' that daylight war so far behind time, I thought creation war in a fair way for freezin' fast.

"So," thinks I, "I must strike a leetle fire from my fingers, light my pipe, travel out a few leagues, and see about it."

Then I brought my knuckles together like two thunder clouds, but the sparks froze up afore I could begin to collect 'em—so out I walked, and endeavored to keep myself unfriz by goin' at a hop, step and jump gait, and whistlin' the tune of "fire in the mountains!" as I went along in three double quick time. Well, arter I had walked about twenty-five miles up the peak o' Daybreak Hill, I soon discovered what war the matter. The airth had actually friz fast in her axis, and couldn't turn round; the sun had got jammed between two cakes o' ice under the wheels, an' thar he had bin shinin' and workin' to get loose, till he friz fast in his cold sweat.

"C-r-e-a-t-i-o-n!" thought I, "this are the toughest sort o' suspension, and it mustn't be endured — somethin' must be done, or human creation is done for."

It war then so anti-deluvian and premature cold that my upper and lower teeth an' tongue war all collapsed together as tight as a friz oyster. I took a fresh twenty pound bear off o' my back that I'd picked up on the road, an' beat the animal agin the ice till the hot ile began to walk out on him at all sides. I then took an' held him over the airth's axes, an' squeezed him till I thaw'd 'em loose, poured about a ton on it over the sun's face, give the airth's cog-wheel one kick backward, till I got the sun loose — whistled "Push along, keep movin'" an' in about fifteen seconds the airth gin a grunt, and begun movin' — the sun walked up beautiful, salutin' me with sich a wind o' gratitude that it made me sneeze. I lit my pipe by the blaze o' his top-knot, shouldered my bear, an' walked home, introducin' the people to fresh daylight with a piece of sunrise in my pocket, with which I cooked my bear steaks, an' enjoyed one o' the best breakfasts I had tasted for some time. If I didn't, just wake some mornin' and go with me to the office o' sunrise!

Another time—he must have been in Arkansas, because people there tell about the thing that happened only a few years back and they can show you the place, too—Davy was bear hunting on Whangdoodle Knob. At sundown, he found he was all played out. He decided to take his rest under a big dead cedar tree. He got to sleep right away, but when he rolled over, he got his powder horn into his ribs. This half waked him, and he took the powder horn off and looked around for a place to hang it. The best place nearby was a yellow limb he saw just above him on the cedar tree, shiny in the moonlight.

The next morning, when he got up, hanged if the powder horn was anywhere in sight or the yellow limb either. It puzzled him all day what had happened to the horn, and he needed it back, too, in order to finish his hunting. That night he figured he'd just go again to the same spot, to see whether he could figure what had happened. When the moon started up, he could see the tree, but the yellow limb still wasn't there. Then the moon—a new moon, by the way—got even with him, and some of it went behind the tree, and the blade was sticking out beyond the tree where he'd thought the yellow limb was, and the powder horn was hanging on the blade.

"Well," says he, "I didn't know Whangdoodle Hill was so high. While I'm this near the moon, guess I'll just hitch a ride. I'll get home quick that way, I expect."

So he vaulted onto the moon and found it, except for the sharp edges, very comfortable. It sailed on up into the sky, and Davy looked down.

"Hey!" says he, at last. "This thing's going west, and the cabin's east of here in Kentucky. Well, it came back tonight, so it'll come back tomorrow. Guess I'll just take the round trip."

So he rode on and on, with the finest view. He crossed the Red River, which he'd seen from that little steamer long before. Then he saw the battered walls of the Alamo, white in the moonlight. He went on across New Mexico and California and then out over the Pacific Ocean. In time, he'd gone around the world and was sailing over the East Coast. From the moon, he managed to glimpse Baltimore, where he'd almost gone to sea, and Washington, where he'd served in Congress. He saw some of the places in Tennessee where he'd lived so long. When the moon got over the Crockett cabin, he flipped off with his powder horn and his rifle Old Betsy and went in to supper.

CONGRESSMAN CROCKETT'S SPEECH ON INDIAN REMOVAL

A Report on the Remarks Made in The House of Representatives, May 19, 1830.

Mr. Crockett said that, considering his very humble abilities, it might be expected that he should content himself with a silent vote; but, situated as he was, in relation to his colleagues, he felt it to be a duty to himself to explain the motives which governed him in the vote he should give on this bill. Gentlemen had already discussed the treaty-making power; and had done it much more ably than he could pretend to do. He should not therefore enter on that subject, but would merely make an explanation as to the reasons of his vote. He did not know whether a man * within 500 miles of his residence

---

*That is, a member of Congress.

would give a similar vote; but he knew, at the same time, that he should give that vote with a clear conscience. He had his constituents to settle with, he was aware; and should like to please them as well as other gentlemen; but he had also a settlement to make at the bar of his God; and what his conscience dictated to be just and right he would do, be the consequences what they might. He believed that the people who had been kind enough to give him their suffrages, supposed him to be an honest man, or they would not have chosen him. If so, they could not but expect that he should act in the way he thought honest and right. He had always viewed the native Indian tribes of this country as a sovereign people. He believed they had been recognized as such from the very foundation of this government, and the United States were bound by treaty to protect them; it was their duty to do so. And as to giving the money of the American people for the purpose of removing them in the manner proposed, he would not do it. He would do that only for which he could answer to his God. Whether he could answer it before the people was comparatively nothing, though it was a great satisfaction to him to have the approbation of his constituents.

Mr. C. said he had served for seven years in a legislative body. But from the first hour he had entered a legislative hall, he had never known what party was in legislation; and God forbid he ever should. He went for the good of the country, and for that only. What he did as a legislator, he did conscientiously. He should love to go with his colleagues, and with the West and the South generally, if he could; but he never would let party govern him in a question of this great consequence.

He had many objections to the bill—some of them of a very serious character. One was, that he did not like to put half a million of money into the hands of the Executive, to be used in a manner which nobody could foresee, and which Congress was not to control. Another objection was, he did not wish to depart from the role which had been observed towards the Indian nations from the foundation of the government. He considered the present application as the last alternative for these poor remnants of a once powerful people. Their only chance of aid was at the hands of Congress. Should its members turn a deaf ear to their cries, misery must be their fate. That was his candid opinion.

Mr. C. said he was often forcibly reminded of the remark made by the famous *Red Jacket*, in the rotundo of this building, when he was shown the pannel which represented in sculpture the first landing of the Pilgrims, with an Indian chief presenting to them an ear of corn, in token of friendly welcome. The aged Indian said "that was good." The Indian said he knew that they came from the Great Spirit, and he was willing to share the soil with his brothers from over the great water. But when he turned round to another pannel representing Penn's treaty, he said "Ah! all's gone now." There was a great deal of truth in this short saying; and the present bill was a strong commentary upon it.

Mr. C. said that four counties of his district bordered on the Chickasaw country. He knew many of their tribe; and nothing should ever induce him to vote to drive them west of the Mississippi. He did not know what sort of a country it was in which they were settled. He would willingly appropriate money in order to send proper persons to examine the country. And when this had been done, and a fair and free treaty had been made with the tribes, if they were desirous of removing, he would vote an appropriation of any sum necessary; but till this had been done, he would not vote one cent. He could not clearly understand the extent of this bill. It seemed to go to the removal of all the Indians, in any State east of the Mississippi river, in which the United States owned any land. Now, there was a considerable number of them still neglected; there was a considerable number of them in Tennessee, and the United

States' government owned no land in that State, north and east of the congressional reservation line. No man could be more willing to see them remove than he was, if it could be done in a manner agreeable to themselves; but not otherwise. He knew personally that a part of the tribe of the Cherokees were unwilling to go. When the proposal was made to them, they said, "No: we will take death here at our homes. Let them come and tomahawk us here at home: we are willing to die, but never to remove." He had heard them use this language. Many different constructions might be put upon this bill. One of the first things which had set him against the bill was the letter from the secretary of war to colonel Mont gomery—from which it appeared that the Indians had been intruded upon. Orders had been issued to turn them all off except the heads of the Indian families, or such as possessed improvements. Government had taken measures to purchase land from the Indians who had gone to Arkansas. If this bill should pass, the same plan would be carried further; they would send and buy them out, and put white men upon their land. It had never been known that white men and Indians could live together; and in this case, the Indians were to have no privileges allowed them, while the white men were to have all. Now, if this was not oppression with a vengeance, he did not know what was. It was the language of the bill, and of its friends, that the Indians were not to be driven off against their will. He knew the Indians were unwilling to go: and therefore he could not consent to place them in a situation where they would be obliged to go. He could not stand that. He knew that he stood alone, having, perhaps, none of his colleagues from his state agreeing in sentiment. He could not help that. He knew that he should return to his home glad and light in heart, if he voted against the bill. He felt that it was his wish and purpose to serve his constituents honestly, according to the light of his conscience. The moment he should exchange his conscience for mere party views, he hoped his Maker would no longer suffer him to exist. He spoke the truth in saying so. If he should be the only member of that House who voted against the bill, and the only man in the United States who disapproved it, he would still vote against it; and it would be matter of rejoicing to him till the day he died, that he had given the vote. He had been told that he should be prostrated; but if so, he would have the consolation of conscience. He would obey that power, and gloried in the deed. He cared not for popularity, unless it could be obtained by upright means. He had seen much to disgust him here; and he did not wish to represent his fellow-citizens, unless he could be permitted to act conscientiously. He had been told that he did not understand English grammar. That was very true. He had never been six months at school in his life: he had raised himself by the labor of his hands. But he did not, on that account, yield up his privilege as the representative of freemen on this floor.* Humble as he was, he meant to exercise his privilege. He had been charged with not representing his constituents. If the fact were so, the error (said Mr. C.) is here (touching his head), not here (laying his hand upon his heart). He never had possessed wealth or education, but he had ever been animated by an independent spirit; and he trusted to prove it on the present occasion.

From *Speeches on the Passage of the Bill for the Removal of the Indians, Delivered in the Congress of the United States, April and May, 1830*. Boston: Perkins and Marvin, 1830. New York: Jonathan Leavitt, 1830. (This volume was supplied by Franklin J. Meine, Editor, American Peoples Encyclopedia.)

---

*Colonel Crockett represents more voters than any member of Congress, except Mr. Duncan of Illinois. The reason is, the great influx of population since the State was formed into districts. There were 20,000 voters in Colonel Crockett's district more than a year ago. There are probably more than 22,000 now.

BIOGRAPHY AND LEGEND

As the Introduction says, this book is about both a historical Davy Crockett (1786-1836) and a legendary David Crockett who was born when the frontiersman was alive, who was nourished over the years after the real man's death, and who still is living. A few words, now, about the sources of what this book has said about each.

Three books which appeared during the 1830's were partly based upon interviews with Crockett, factual news stories about him, or upon his writings. *Sketches and Eccentricities of Col. Davy Crockett of West Tennessee* (1833), by Mathew St. Clair Clarke, although it wasn't written with Crockett's overt help or with his approval, made use of stories Crockett had told and of newspaper accounts. *A Narrative of the Life of Colonel David Crockett of the State of Tennessee Written By Himself* (1834) is the book that best deserves to be called an autobiography, since it was written by Crockett in collaboration with Thomas Chilton. *An Account of Colonel Crockett's Tour to the North and Down East* (1835), though it was published by the Whigs as propaganda and its author probably was William Clark, made use of newspaper reports

189

and of some notes furnished by Crockett. I have utilized these for factual accounts with caution, and frequently have quoted phrasings since I'm convinced that they often faithfuly echo Crockett's way of talking. Other reliable sources include Crockett's letters, the Register of the Debates in Congress, Vols. IV-VI and X-XI, and "Sketch of the Remarks of David Crockett on the Bill for the Removal of the Indians, Made May 19, 1830," in a rare book, *Speeches on the Passage of the Bill for the Removal of the Indians . . .* (1830).

For another book that was claimed to be by Crockett— *Colonel Crockett's Exploits and Adventures in Texas…Written by Himself* (1836), Crockett evidently furnished matter used in the first two chapters, though the author actually was Richard Penn Smith. The book is valuable chiefly for those initial chapters and the contemporary material that it contains, including a report concerning its subject's death that is nearer to being correct than the account that was credited for many years. The source of this essentially accurate version apparently was a letter written to the New York *Courier and Enquirer* from Galveston Bay in June, 1836, by a correspondent who had interviewed a Mexican soldier who had been an eye witness.

Biographies which tell about the historical Crockett and which I have drawn upon are those by James J. Roche, E. S. Ellis, William C. Sprague, Marcus J. Wright, Constance Rourke, and—most confidently— the superb study by James A. Shackford, *David Crockett: The Man and the Legend* (1956), edited and published after the author's death by a brother, John B. Shackford. A. P. Foster, "David Crockett," *Tennessee Historical Magazine* (1925) and was useful. I tried to clear up some confusions about Crockett in an article, "Six Davy Crocketts," in *The Southwest Review*, 1940, which became a chapter of my book, *Horse Sense in American Humor*, in 1942.

Material on the historical Crockett in Tennessee has been drawn from T. P. Abernethy, *Frontier to Plantation in Tennessee*; Ray Allen Billington, *Westward Expansion*; Donald Davidson, *The Tennessee River*; Timothy Flint, *Recollections of the Last Ten Years*; Joseph C. Guild, *Old Times in Tennessee*; John Haywood, *The Civil and Political History of Tennessee*; John T. Moore and Austin P. Foster, *Tennessee, the Volunteer State*; and Samuel Cole Williams, *Beginnings of West Tennessee in the Land of the Chickasaws*.

Books which deal with the Creek War and Crockett in Congress are: Grant Foreman, *Indian Removal*; Henry S. Halpert and Timothy H. Ball, *The Creek War*; Marquis James, *Andrew Jackson, the Border Captain*; and James Parton, *Life of Andrew Jackson*, 3 volumes.

Several books have been useful for the historical account of Crockett's trip to Texas and the siege of the Alamo: H. H. Bancroft, *History of the North Mexican States and Texas*; Eugene C. Barker, *Mexico and Texas*, 1831-1835: James R. Masterson, *Tall Tales of Arkansas*; John M. Myers, *The Alamo*; and Justin H. Smith, *The Annexation of Texas and the War with Mexico*, in two volumes. For years, the most useful study of the siege was a series of four articles by Amelia Williams, "A Critical Study of the Siege of the Alamo and of the Personnel of Its Defenders," published in *The Southwestern Historical Quarterly* in 1933. Although these continue to be valuable, some studies published between 1975 and 1980 convincingly argue for an important revision of the account of Crockett's death. Three books provide the evidence: José Enrique de la Peña, *With Santa Anna in Texas: A Personal Narrative of the Revolution*, translated and edited by Car-

191

men Perry (1975); Dan Kilgore, *How Did Davy Die?* (1978); and Francisco Becarra, *A Mexican Sergeant's Recollections of the Alamo and San Jacinto, as Told to John S. Ford in 1875*, edited by Dan Kilgore (1980).

I have also drawn upon the newspapers of Crockett's time, the *Boston Transcript*, *Washington Globe*, *New York Times*, and a few others.

The newspapers told about not only the historical David Crockett but also, on occasion, about the legendary Davy Crockett: many anecdotes and tall stories going the rounds during the man's lifetime and some years after his death were published in them. Great numbers of stories were included in various *Crockett Almanacs* and *Almanacks* published between 1834 and 1855, credited to publishers in Nashville, New York, Philadelphia, and Boston. The so-called Nashville almanacs for 1835, 1836, 1837, and 1838 contained claims that Crockett had furnished their material and that Crockett or his family backed their publication. This claim is doubtful, and John Seelye, in "The Well-Wrought Crockett," *Toward a New American Literary History* (1980) presents an argument on the basis of strong circumstantial evidence that these weren't published in Nashville but in Boston. He concludes that therefore Eastern journalists must have been the creators of many of the tall tales about Crockett that appeared in the almanacs: this likelihood had been indicated by James Shackford, Joseph Arpad, and others. I have used the almanacs made available by Franklin J. Meine; as well as his edition of those with the Nashville imprint, privately printed by the Caxton Club in 1955. I have also used a collection of some of the best, *Davy Crockett: American Comic Legend*, ed. Richard M. Dorson (1939). Joseph Leach's *The Typical Texan* contains others: it also offers a useful list of the different almanacs along with the names of libraries which have them. Recent stories about Crockett are told in Vance Randolph's *Ozark Mountain Folks*. I have encountered others in travel books, humorous books and in publications of folklore organizations, the Tennessee Folklore Society and in particular the Texas Folklore Society.

For background as well as for legends, I have drawn upon the publications I have listed above. In addition, I have made use of many of the writings of a group of humorists who wrote authentically about life in the South and the Southwest in Crockett's day.

Selection from Crockett's
FREE-AND-EASY
SONG BOOK. — 1837

THE ALAMO, OR THE DEATH OF
CROCKETT.

BY R. T. CONRAD, ESQUIRE.
Air—Star-Spangled Banner

To the memory of Crockett fill up to the brim!
>The hunter, the hero, the bold yankee yeoman!
Let the flowing oblation be poured forth to him
>>Who ne'er turned his back on his friend or his foeman
>>>And grateful shall be
>>>His fame to the free;
Fill! fill! to the brave who for Liberty bled —
May his name and his fame to the last — GO AHEAD!

When the Mexicans leaguered thy walls, Alamo!
>'Twas Crockett looked down on the war-storm's com-
>motion,
And smiled, as by thousands the foe spread below,
>>And rolled o'er the plain, like the waves of the ocean.
>>>The Texans stood there —
>>>Their flag fanned the air,
>>>And their shout bade the foe try what freemen will
>>>dare.
What recked they, tho' thousands the prairies o'erspread?
The word of their leader was still — GO AHEAD

194

They came! Like the sea-cliff that laughs at the flood,
    Stood that dread band of heroes the onslaught repelling;
Again! And again! yet undaunted they stood;
    While Crocket's deep voice o'er the wild din was swel-
    ling.
        "Go ahead!" was his cry,
        "Let us conquer or die;
        "And shame to the wretch and the dastard who'd fly!"
And still, mid the battle-cloud, lurid and red,
Rang the hero's dread cry — *Go ahead!* GO AHEAD!

He fought — but no valour that horde could withstand;
    He fell — but behold where the wan victor found him!
With a smile on his lip, and his rifle in hand,
    He lay, with his foemen heaped redly around him;
        His heart poured its tide
        In the cause of its pride,
        A freeman he lived, and a freeman he died;
For liberty struggled, for liberty bled —
May his name and his fame to the last — GO AHEAD!

Then fill up to Crockett — fill up to the brim!
    The hunter, the hero, the bold yankee yeoman!
Let the flowing oblation be poured forth to him,
    Who ne'er turned his back on his friend or his foeman!
        And grateful shall be
        His fame to the free,
        For a bolder or better they never shall see.
Fill! fill! to the brave who for Liberty bled —
May his name and his fame to the last — GO AHEAD!